research techniques for
program planning, monitoring, and evaluation

IRWIN EPSTEIN and TONY TRIPODI

NEW YORK ▪ COLUMBIA UNIVERSITY PRESS

Library of Congress Cataloging in Publication Data

Epstein, Irwin.
Research techniques for program planning, monitoring,
and evaluation.

Includes bibliographies and index.
1. Social service—Research—United States.
2. Evaluation research (Social action programs)
I. Tripodi, Tony, joint author.   II. Title.
HV95.E67   361'.007'2073   76-51825
ISBN 0-231-03944-1

Columbia University Press
New York   Guildford, Surrey

Printed in the United States of America

10 9 8 7 6 5 4 3 2

To
Joseph H. Epstein,
Rae L. Epstein,
and
Roni Tripodi

Acknowledgments

WE WISH TO THANK Phillip Fellin, Dean of the University of Michigan School of Social Work for his encouragement and for provision of time and clerical resources. In addition, we are indebted to Helen Colby-Bernstein, Margaret Lemley, and Marilyn Moore for their work on the original manuscript.

IRWIN EPSTEIN
TONY TRIPODI

Contents

research techniques for
program planning,
monitoring,
and evaluation

CHAPTER ONE

Introduction

THE PURPOSE OF THIS BOOK is to provide an introduction to the administrative uses of research. It is written for people who are not research trained. It is neither a comprehensive social research text nor an auditor's guide to fiscal administration. Broadly, our intention is to show how research concepts and techniques can be utilized by program planners and administrators in developing, maintaining, and modifying social programs. Special emphasis is given to the application of research techniques to program planning, monitoring, and evaluation. The book offers a range of techniques that can be easily understood by administrators and planners with a minimal research background.

WHY WE WROTE THE BOOK

Many program administrators and planners have not had adequate training in the administrative uses of research. Despite this lack, they face increasing pressure from potential funding sources, professional groups and recipients of service to provide and to make use of systematic research data. Moreover, sound professional practice requires that program administrators be more rational and objective in planning, monitoring, and evaluating their programs. Research facilitates rationality; it provides information that is essential for responsible administrative decision making. From a pragmatic point of view, research has become an important element in funding proposals because of reduced funding opportunities and increased competition among social programs.

Until recently, administrators and planners relied on research consultants to assist them in performing necessary research tasks. However, for several reasons, this practice proved too costly, and frequently it did not serve administrative or programmatic needs. First, a considerable amount of time was required to acquaint the consultant with program means and objectives. Second, staff often presented obstacles to the consultant's entry into the program, subverted efforts at data collection, or distorted research findings. Third, the consultant's research orientation was often incompatible with the information requirements or financial resources of the program. Fourth, a rigid, experimental research orientation required the denial of service to a control population, which was ethically and professionally unacceptable to practitioners. Finally, information feedback was often too slow, and when it came it was couched in language that was not directly applicable to programmatic decision making.

This book is intended to provide research skills that will assist administrators *directly* in making program decisions. Of course, carrying out highly sophisticated research studies depends on extensive experience in doing research; and it is not expected that a reading of this book will enable one to function as a seasoned researcher. However, we believe that the book provides administrators and students of administration with a realistic sense of the uses of research techniques for increasing the quality and effectiveness of administrative practice. Hopefully, these techniques will lessen dependency on costly research consultation. If not, our hope is that the book will increase the accountability of outside research consultants or inside research staff to a more sophisticated administrative clientele.

INTENDED AUDIENCE

The book is addressed to administrators and planners of health, education, and social welfare programs with goals of individual or social betterment. It is also designed to serve as a textbook for administrative, planning, and evaluation research courses in schools of social work, education, public administration, and public health. It can be used as a supplementary text in more basic courses in research, planning, and administration.

Our working assumption is that the present and future practitioners who use this text will do so in the best service traditions of their respective professions—not simply for organizational maintenance or aggrandizement. While we recognize that programs must survive if they are to serve, our emphasis is on the use of research to provide the best possible service to agency clientele.

FORMAT

The book is organized into three major sections: program planning, monitoring, and evaluation. Each section begins with a description of the administrative function to which it is devoted, followed by a set of selected research techniques. To facilitate the use of these techniques, each chapter will contain a general description of a technique, a hypothetical case illustration of its use, and an exercise for the reader in applying the technique in an existing social program or agency.

It should be emphasized that the range of research techniques and applications presented is not exhaustive. We have selected only those that we feel are appropriate for administrators and planners with limited background and experience in research. Moreover, though we apply specific techniques to particular functions, there is no reason to assume that these techniques should be confined to the planning, monitoring, or evaluation contexts in which they are introduced. Throughout the book, we argue for the broader applicability of these research techniques in administrative decision making.

PART ONE

PROGRAM PLANNING

IN ITS BROADEST SENSE, planning is the process by which society addresses social problems. Frequently, this process involves creating new social agencies and the resources to maintain them. In this book, however, we conceive of planning more narrowly. Our discussion is limited to the program planning functions of administrators in *existing* social agencies with *committed* sources of funding.

Once an administrator has an idea for a new agency program, he requires valid and reliable information concerning (1) the potential target population, its characteristics and its needs; (2) existing programs to meet these needs, as well as the location of existing resources that could enhance the operation of a new program; (3) specific intervention strategies, technologies, or services that are known to be relatively effective and efficient in meeting needs of the target population; (4) the skills of agency staff. Sometimes this information is already available to the administrator. More frequently, data must be collected.

The need for such information persists throughout the life of a program, so that program planning is closely related to monitoring and evaluation. By monitoring and evaluating a developing program, an administrator can determine the extent to which the program is serving the need to which it was originally addressed and the extent to which the need persists. Judgments can also be made about the relation between the program and changing patterns of service within the community, raising questions about interagency coordination of services. As techniques of intervention and service delivery evolve, the administrator will want to keep abreast of these changes and make appropriate modifications in the program. Finally, judgments about the individual and collective competencies of program staff are an integral part of administrative practice. Thus, although program planning is critical in the initiation of a social program, in many respects it is a continuous process based on the systematic feedback of accurate information.

ADMINISTRATIVE DECISIONS IN PROGRAM PLANNING

Planning requires that specific decisions be made about the initiation and continuous operation of a program. More specifically, program initiation involves decision making in the following primary areas: procurement of the necessary material, professional, technological, and social resources; recruitment of clientele; assessment of staff competency and training needs; allocation of staff and resources; articulation of the proposed program in terms of overall agency objectives; and coordination of the program with others in the community. Needless to say, these decisions must be made in the context of an operating budget. Budgetary constraints must be considered in planning for the volume of clients to be served, the geographic boundaries from which they will be recruited, and eligibility criteria, so that realistic objectives can be set for relating potential client "demand" to the available "supply" of services.

Planning for a new program requires, in addition to consideration of agency resources, a knowledge of existing resources outside the agency. Careful consideration of other existing programs may lead to (1) a decision that a new program is unnecessary; (2) the development of a referral system directing agency clientele to existing programs; (3) the development of a new program patterned after another successful program in the community; or (4) the development of a totally new program.

In choosing specific intervention strategies, patterns of service delivery, or therapeutic technologies, the administrator requires sound information about the comparative effectiveness and efficiency of different program strategies. How would they affect client attitudes, knowledge, behaviors, satisfaction, and the like? What is the experience of other programs that have implemented such strategies? How do the strategies mesh with the particular needs of the target population addressed by the new program?

Other planning decisions involve judgments about whether agency staff require in-service training and supervision for the performance of new tasks. Some tasks may involve training outside the agency or the hiring of new personnel.

The significance of the foregoing decisions may vary from program to program, or from time to time within a program. As objectives are realized or as they shift, the administrator is involved in decisions about changing priorities. These decisions may be made by the administrator alone or in collaboration with planning boards, staff, client groups, funding sources, and so on. Hence programs are continually changing, as are the organizational environments in which they are embedded. Objectives change as the needs of target populations change. Sources of support dry up or expand. New funding sources appear. Technologies evolve. Values change. Essentially, then, planning is a dynamic process that can benefit from a continuing flow of information from the program itself and its surrounding environment.

RESEARCH TECHNIQUES AND PROGRAM PLANNING

Research techniques can be usefully employed to satisfy many of the information requirements of program planning. Once a program has been initiated, they can provide the kinds of information necessary for program maintenance or modification through monitoring and evaluation techniques. In this section, however, our immediate focus is on research concepts and techniques applied to planning decisions.

Questionnaires, for example, are useful for securing information from potential clients, practicing professionals, and other concerned people about target population's needs, its use of existing programs, and the kinds of new services to which it is likely to respond. Questionnnaires are useful as well for determining the success or failure of existing programs dealing with a particular problem or population group. This information would be helpful in coordinating efforts of existing programs with a new program and in selecting intervention strategies. A questionnaire may also be administered to agency staff to determine the adequacy of their professional training for a new program or set of interventions.

The next chapter is devoted to the principles of questionnaire construction. Although questionnaires can be used to generate reliable and valid information about a whole range of planning decisions, they are useful in program monitoring and evaluation as well. For purposes of illustration, however, we will demonstrate how this powerful research technique can be used to provide information about the needs of a particular target population and its potential use of a new social program.

In chapter 3 another research technique is introduced—the interview. In that chapter, we will discuss principles of interviewing and illustrate the technique by showing how semistructured interviews conducted with agency administrators and executives may be used to obtain information about existing programs. Here again, the research technique is applicable to a whole range of needs. Whatever the decision making context, however, the principles of good interviewing remain the same.

In planning a new program, an effective administrator will want to make use of information that is already available in the form of research literature, census reports, agency evaluations, and the like. Chapter 4 is written to facilitate the effective use of such information. In that chapter, we focus on criteria for assessing available information. More specifically, we show how research reports can be used to assess the effectiveness and efficiency of various intervention strategies. This information is essential to the rational selection of program technologies and to realistic setting of program objectives.

In chapter 5, observational techniques are discussed. To illustrate the use of systematic observation, we focus on the way in which it can aid in determining staff training and supervisory needs. It should be remembered, however, that questionnaires, interviews, and available personnel information may also be used to shed light on staff training needs.

SELECTED BIBLIOGRAPHY

Freeman, Howard E., and Clarence C. Sherwood. *Social Research and Social Policy*. Englewood Cliffs, N.J.: Prentice-Hall, 1970.

Kahn, Alfred J. *Theory and Practice of Social Planning*. New York: Russell Sage Foundation, 1969.

Massie, Joseph L. *Essentials of Management*. 2d ed. Englewood Cliffs, N.J.: Prentice-Hall, 1971; pp. 82–92.

Morris, Robert, and Robert H. Binstock, with Martin Rein. *Feasible Planning for Social Change*. New York: Columbia University Press, 1966.

Schatz, Harry A., ed. *Social Work Administration: A Resource Book*. New York: Council on Social Work Education, 1970.

Terry, George R. *Principles of Management*. 6th ed. Homewood, Ill.: Richard D. Irwin, 1972; pp. 191–296.

CHAPTER TWO

Constructing Questionnaires for Need-Assessment Surveys

QUESTIONNAIRES ARE PROBABLY the most commonly used data-gathering instruments. Their primary purpose is to obtain facts and opinions about a phenomenon from knowledgeable respondents. Social researchers have employed questionnaires in everything from national opinion polls to case studies to laboratory experiments. Frequently, social program administrators use them as well.

The versatility of questionnaires is further demonstrated by the many different ways in which they can be administered. They may be mailed to respondents and self-administered. They may be administered by someone other than the respondent, in which case questions are read to the respondent and answers recorded by the interviewer. They can be administered to groups as well as to individuals. However, although questionnaires are versatile, they can be successfully employed *only* when respondents are literate, motivated to read and answer questions carefully, and knowledgeable about the matters covered in the questions.

A well-constructed questionnaire presents the respondent with a clear set of instructions about how to answer the questions, that is, a response system. The response system may be *open-ended*. In this type of system, a blank space is left after the question for the respondent to write in his or her answers. Or, responses may be *closed,* or *forced-choice*. Responses in this system are prestructured; the respondent is required to check appropriate response categories. Many questionnaires have a mix of closed and open-ended questions.

QUESTIONNAIRES AND SOCIAL PROGRAM ADMINISTRATION

Questionnaires are useful for gathering information relevant to all aspects of social program administration. With respect to program planning, for example, questionnaires may be used to ascertain from potential clients the extent and type of their service needs, their current knowledge and use of existing programs, and their estimates regarding their participation in newly proposed programs. With regard to program monitoring, questionnaires are frequently used to gain information about how staff is allocating its efforts. In program evaluation, questionnaires can be used to ask administrators, program staff, and clientele about their subjective evaluations of social programs. In this chapter, we present some basic principles of questionnaire construction and illustrate the use of questionnaires in the conduct of need-assessment surveys.

PRINCIPLES OF QUESTIONNAIRE CONSTRUCTION

1. The Purpose of the Questionnaire

In constructing a questionnaire, one should be clear about the reasons for wanting to use it, the kind of information to be gathered, and the population to whom the questionnaire is addressed. One must decide whether the population can understand the questions and has sufficient knowledge to answer them. In addition, one should be able to describe clearly why the information is desired, why the respondent is being asked to participate, and how the information will be utilized. This should be done in a few brief introductory sentences so that potential respondents can make an informed choice as to whether to participate.

Respondents will usually participate if they believe they are knowledgeable about the area of inquiry and feel confident that the information gathered will not be used to hurt them and will be put to good use. People are least reluctant to respond to questionnaires when they can be assured that their responses will remain anonymous.

2. The Information to Be Gathered

Before constructing questions or deciding on a response system, one should list the types of information desired. For example, in the construction of a need-assessment survey such a list might include personal information, present use of social programs, knowledge of community resources, dissatisfactions with current services received, unmet needs, and so on.

The purpose of such a list is to insure that the questionnaire covers the range of information desired in the most economical form. This is important, because it is difficult and costly to go back and resurvey respondents if important information was left out of the original questionnaire. It is equally important, however, that essential information be gathered in the shortest possible time. People will not respond to or will lose interest in a questionnaire that is too long. *Ideally, completion time should not exceed one-half hour*.

Accordingly, one should go over the list of areas and narrow it down to those that are most important and potentially useful. For example, an administrator of a family service agency may be generally interested in the abuse of drugs and alcohol in his client population, their health needs, life aspirations, and so on; but the most immediate problem facing the agency might be whether to institute a new homemaker service for which federal funds are suddenly available. Rather than using a single questionnaire to serve all purposes, it would be more efficient to devise a relatively simple, short questionnaire that is likely to yield a good response rate and reliable information, and that can be quickly analyzed to inform decision making about the homemaker service.

3. The Format of the Questionnaire

In considering the format of a proposed questionnaire, one must decide whether the questionnaire will be self-administered or not, where and under what conditions respondents will complete the questionnaire, and how it will be returned. Generally speaking, the higher the respondents' level of education, motivation, involvement in the issues covered, and so on, the more successful a self-administered, mailed questionnaire will be.

To begin with, the format should include a brief description of purpose, how the information will be used, what provisions have been made for assuring anonymity, and so on. Sometimes the endorsements of agencies or individuals who are important to respondents will facilitate a high response rate.

Then the response system must be chosen. Should questions be open-ended or closed? Open-ended questions require less advance knowledge about the kinds of responses that questions are likely to elicit. They are most useful for covering areas in which there is little previous information and in which response categories are difficult to anticipate. However, responses to them take a great deal of time to analyze and to summarize. These questions highlight the variability in responses. Closed questions are preferable for simple data processing. They lend themselves easily to counting and percentaging. However, they require a good deal of knowledge about the kinds of responses one is likely to get. If the precoded categories are wrong, important information is irretrievably lost. Most commonly, questionnaires have some combination of open-ended and closed questions.

The following list indicates the range of response types available for what is basically the same question.

a. The open-ended question:

In what ways would a homemaker be most useful to your family?

(write in) _____

_____

_____

_____

b. Closed questions:

1. Simple "yes" or "no."

    Would a homemaker be helpful to you in dealing with your current family problems? Yes_____ No_____

2. "Agree"/"disagree" scales.

    Indicate how much you agree or disagree with the following statement:

    A homemaker would be helpful to me in dealing with my current family problems. (check one)

    Strongly   Strongly
    Agree_____ Agree_____ Disagree_____ Disagree_____

3. Frequency of response scales (adverb modifiers).

    If a homemaker were available, how frequently would you need her services? (check one)

    Frequently_____ Occasionally_____ Never_____

4. Frequency of response scales (numerical).

    If a homemaker were available to you, on how many days of the week would you need her services? (check one)

Three or   One or
Seven_____   Six_____   Five_____   Four_____   Two_____   None_____

5. Frequency of response scales (percentage).

   If a homemaker were available to you, what percentage of your family problems would be solved? (check one)

   75–100%_____   50–74%_____   25–49%_____   0–24%_____

6. Comparative response scales.

   Compared to other services you currently need how important is homemaker services? (check one)

   Very Important_____   Somewhat Important_____   Unimportant_____

7. Identification response.

   Below is a list of ways in which a homemaker could be helpful to you. Please check those areas in which you could most use her help. (check as many as apply)

   Help with housecleaning   _____
   Help with budgeting   _____
   Help with child management   _____
   Help with preparing meals   _____

Just as questionnaires may contain a mix of open-ended and closed questions, the questions themselves may contain aspects of both. For example, item 7 above can be supplemented with blank lines set aside for the respondent to write in uses that are not already listed.

Whatever the response system chosen, however, response categories should be mutually exclusive. This means that for any given question, the answer must fit into one and only one response category. In other words, the categories may not overlap. In addition, they should exhaust the range of possible responses. Finally, wherever possible, one should avoid the use of "Don't know," "Undecided," "Does not apply," and other such noncommittal categories. These response categories discourage thoughtful deliberation on the part of the respondent in answering difficult questions. When they are overused by the respondents, they may also indicate ambiguous questions.

In constructing a questionnaire, it is preferable to choose one or two types of response that are readily understood by respondents. Excessive variation of the response system leads to confusion, fatigue, and unreliable information.

For each series of questions that involve a specific type of response, there should be instructions as to the manner in which the respondent should answer the questions. Personal information questions should go at the end of the questionnaire, after the more substantive questions. Overall, the sequence of questions should follow a logical order with appropriate transitions so that the respondent will want to complete it.

4. Writing the Questions

In writing questions, one should follow three general principles: (1) questions and response alternatives should be clear; (2) questions and response alternatives should not reflect biases of the questioner; (3) each question should contain one thought only. Moreover, the vocabulary and syntax of the questionnaire should correspond to that of the respondent population. The art of asking questions is to ask them simply and concisely in understandable language, so that unbiased responses can be obtained. In order to insure that questions make sense to and are answerable by respondents, a pretest of the questionnaire is essential.

5. Pretesting the Questionnaire

While constructing questions, one may try them out on colleagues who are familiar with the respondent population. But to get a good working idea of the questionnaire's usefulness one should try it out on a small sample of the population for which it is intended. After obtaining answers from the respondents and finding out how long it took them to complete the questionnaire, one should attempt to find out whether any questions were unclear or difficult to interpret, whether the questionnaire was fatiguing, and finally whether there were questions or response categories relevant to the inquiry that were not included in the questionnaire.

The pretest serves to clarify ambiguous questions, eliminate unnecessary or biased questions, and in general to determine the feasibility of the questionnaire.

6. Administering the Questionnaire

When the questionnaire is ready for use, one must consider ways in which to facilitate an acceptable response rate, that is, 65 percent or more. For mailed questionnaires, one should enclose a covering letter explaining the purpose of the study and an addressed, stamped return envelope. Follow-up letters or postcards should be sent out two to three weeks after the original mailing to encourage those who have not completed the questionnaire to do so. A second follow-up reminder might be sent after another two-week period. Telephone follow-ups might also be considered.

Another strategy is to hand deliver questionnaires at suitable locations. Applicants for agency service might be given a questionnaire while they are waiting for their intake appointments and instructed to hand it to a receptionist when they have completed it. Parents at a PTA meeting might receive a questionnaire at the meeting and be given time to answer it. If the questionnaire is designed for employees, time could be set aside for completion during their workday.

Hypothetical Illustration

PROBLEM SITUATION AND ADMINISTRATIVE TASK

An administrator of a public welfare agency is interested in whether or not new day care facilitites should be developed in the community for public welfare recipients. The administrator may already know what day care facilities are currently available and the extent to which they are utilized. If there is additional need, he can purchase day care services through available welfare funds. The problem is one of locating the extent and type of need. A decision is made to survey agency clientele to determine their day care needs and their present child care arrangements. In addition, the administrator would like to know whether the provision of additional day care services would free a significant number of welfare recipients to participate in vocational training, further education, or employment. After the questionnaire is developed and pretested it will be given to agency clientele during their routine contacts with social workers.

DESIGNING AND PRETESTING THE QUESTIONNAIRE

1. The Purpose of the Questionnaire

Once the general problem has been identified, the purpose of the questionnaire must be specified. In this illustration, the purpose of the questionnaire is to estimate the proportion of public welfare recipients with pre-school-aged children who could benefit from additional day care service. In addition, one would want to know whether use of additional services would facilitate vocational training, further education, or employment.

2. Information to Be Gathered

Once the purpose has been specified, one should decide on the general areas of information required. In this case, the areas considered most important are: number of preschool children; past and present use of day care facilities; alternative child care arrangements; hours during which child care is most needed; willingness to participate in day care program activities; attitudes about the purposes of day care, for example, simple babysitting, educational, purposes, and so on.

3. The Format of the Questionnaire

It is decided that the questionnaire should contain mostly simple closed questions that can be answered and analyzed quickly. A covering letter and introduction would look something like this:

Dear _____

We are trying to find out whether you could use help with child care and if so, what kinds of day care services would be most useful to you.

Please complete this brief questionnaire and return it to your social worker. Your answers will be kept confidential. They will not effect your eligibility for public welfare or the level of your benefits.

Thank you for your cooperation.

Sincerely,

4. Writing the Questions

Some of the questions might look something like this:

1. How many children do you have living with you? (check one)

    0____   1____   2____   3____   4____   5 or more____

2. How many of the children living with you are between 2 and 6 years old? (check one)

    0____   1____   2____   3____   4____   5 or more____

3. Have your children attended a day care center before? (check one)

    Yes____   No____

4. If your children have attended a day care center before, was it in your present community? (check one)

Yes____ No____

5. What current child care arrangements do you have? (check the one which you use most often)

____a. None
____b. Day care center in community
____c. Day care center outside the community
____d. Older children babysit
____e. Outside babysitter
____f. Leave children with friends outside the house
____g. Other (please write in) _____
        _____
        _____

6. If a day care center were available to you, how many days a week would you use it for your children? (check one)

0____   1____   2____   3____   4____   5____   6____   7____

7. At what times would you be most likely to use day care services? (check one)

Mornings____ Afternoons____ Mornings and Afternoons____

8. For each of the statements listed below, indicate the extent to which you agree or disagree by checking whether you Strongly Agree, Mildly Agree, Mildly Disagree, or Strongly Disagree.

a. Day care centers should provide educational instruction
   as well as babysitting for the
   children.   SA____ MA____ MD____ SD____

b. Day care centers should provide for nighttime babysit-
   ting.   SA____ MA____ MD____ SD____

c. Parents should participate in
   day care center activities.   SA____ MA____ MD____ SD____

9. If your children attended a day care center, how interested would you be in going back to school? (check one)

Very Interested____ Somewhat Interested____ Not Interested____

10. If your children attended a day care center, how interested would you be in going back to work? (check one)

    Very Interested_____ Somewhat Interested_____ Not Interested_____

11. If your children attended a day care center, how interested would you be in getting some additional job training? (check one)

    Very Interested_____ Somewhat Interested_____ Not Interested_____

Finally, we'd like to ask a few questions about yourself: (check one response for each question)

12. Age: 18 or below_____ 19–25_____ 26–35_____ 36–45_____ Over 46_____

13. Race: White_____ Black_____ Chicano_____ Other_____

14. Marital Status: Married_____ Divorced_____ Separated_____
    Never married_____

5. Pretesting the Questionnaire

The draft of the questionnaire should then be pretested with 10 public welfare recipients to find out whether they understood the questions, how long it took to complete the questionnaire, what information relevant to child care problems was left out, and so on. On the basis of the information gained in the pretest, the questionnaire would be revised and then used.

EXERCISE

In your community, identify two different groups of people that might benefit from a drug treatment program. The groups might include high school students, industrial workers, college students, unemployed workers, and so on.

Construct two questionnaires, one for each group, for the purpose of determining what kinds of drugs are currently being used by these groups, the extent of their use, and the users' desire for treatment.

Pretest each questionnaire with 5 to 10 respondents from each group. From the pretest develop either a single questionnaire that can be used for both groups or final versions of separate questionnaires designed to serve the particular needs of each.

SELECTED BIBLIOGRAPHY

Best, John W. *Research in Education*. 2d ed. Englewood Cliffs, N.J.: Prentice-Hall, 1970: pp. 160–86.

Goldstein, Harris K. *Research Standards and Methods for Social Workers*. New Orleans, La.: The Hauser Press, 1963; pp. 135–42.

Isaac, Stephen, with William B. Michael. *Handbook in Research and Evaluation*. San Diego, Cal.: Robert R. Knapp, 1971; pp. 92–99.

Kornhauser, Arthur, and Paul B. Sheatsley. "Questionnaire Construction and Interview Procedure," in Claire Selltiz, Marie Jahoda, Morton Deutsch, and Stuart W. Cook, *Research Methods in Social Relations*. New York: Henry Holt, 1959.

Moser, C. A. *Survey Methods in Social Investigation*. London: Heinemann, 1958; pp. 210–45.

Payne, Stanley L. *The Art of Asking Questions*. Princeton, N.J.: Princeton University Press, 1951.

CHAPTER THREE

Interviewing for Resource Surveys

THE RESEARCH INTERVIEW, like the questionnaire, is a powerful and versatile technique for generating information. Unlike administering a questionnaire, however, interviewing involves a face-to-face exchange between the person seeking information and the person giving it. As a result, successful interviewing requires that the interviewer give a good deal of attention to his role in the interview situation. His goal is to gather relevant data by encouraging, facilitating, and guiding the respondent to provide unbiased answers to questions.

Interviews may vary from relatively *unstructured* formats to *semistructured* to highly *structured* ones. In their most structured form, interviews are simply questionnaires that are read aloud by an interviewer who then records the respondent's answers. In these structured interviews, the interview *schedule* contains explicit instructions for the interviewer as well as specific questions for the respondent. The questions are generally forced-choice questions. Consequently, the structured interview is characterized by a high degree of control over both the interviewer and the respondent.

At the other end of the continuum is the unstructured interview. This technique is best suited for studying highly sensitive or unexplored subjects in depth through the use of open-ended questions. The interviewer is free to rephrase questions and to use whatever supportive or probing comments are necessary to elicit desired information. This technique demands great sensitivity to the respondent's feelings, opinions, and behaviors. The unstructured interview involves little control over the interviewer and respondent.

Somewhere between these extremes is the semistructured interview. It usually involves some combination of open-ended and forced-choice questions. Within specified limits, the interviewer may rephrase questions or probe responses. However, his task is to keep the respondent focused on particular issues and questions. As a result, he exercises more control over the direction of the interview than he would in a less structured situation.

Whatever the type of interview, successful information retrieval requires that respondents understand the questions, be motivated to answer them honestly, and be knowledgeable about the matters covered in the interview. Moreover, the interviewer should conduct himself in a friendly but professional manner and show interest in and knowledge about the topics discussed. Most important, he should be nonjudgmental and accepting of the opinions expressed by the respondent.

INTERVIEWING AND SOCIAL PROGRAM ADMINISTRATION

Like questionnaires, interviews are useful for gathering information relevant to *all* aspects of social program administration. In program planning, for example, interviews may be employed to gather information about those services that currently exist within a community. This information facilitates coordination and discourages duplication of services. In monitoring, interviews are useful for gaining information about reasons for staff noncompliance with agency procedures. In program evaluation, clients may be interviewed about their subjective evaluations of the service received, the current state of the problem for which they received service, and so on. In this chapter, we present some basic principles of interviewing and then illustrate the use of the semistructured interview in the conduct of resource surveys.

PRINCIPLES OF RESEARCH INTERVIEWING

1. The Purpose of the Interview

In planning a research interview, one should be clear about the reasons for wanting to conduct it, the kind of information to be gathered, the population to be interviewed, and the role of the interviewer. In a few brief introductory comments, one should clearly describe the purpose of the interview so that respondents know why the information is desired and how it will be used, and can make an informed choice as to whether to participate. As with questionnaires, respondents are most cooperative when they can be assured of anonymity. Finally, one should consider how much and what kind of interviewer activity will be necessary to achieve the purpose of the interview.

2. The Information to Be Gathered

Before constructing interview questions or making decisions about structure, one should list the types of information desired. For example, in conducting a resource survey interview such a list might include: the relevant services provided by other agencies within the community; success or failure of these services in meeting existing needs; estimates of future needs; plans for expanding, maintaining, or contracting existing service programs; and so on.

The purpose of such a list is to see to it that the interview covers the range of information desired in the shortest possible time. *As a general rule, an interview should not exceed one hour.*

3. The Interview Schedule

The interview schedule has two basic functions: it serves as a guide to the interviewer and poses the questions to the respondent. As an interviewer's guide, it includes an *introduction* in which the interviewer states his organizational auspice, the purpose of the interview, assurance of anonymity, and so on. This helps to establish rapport with the respondent and orients him to the topics covered in the interview.

Although interviews generally contain more open-ended questions than questionnaires do, the basic principles of question writing remain the same. Questions should be clear, unbiased, and each focused on a single thought or issue. The language and syntax of the questions should correspond to that of the respondent. The questions themselves may range from open-ended to the many different kinds of forced-choice items indicated in the preceding chapter.

In an interview situation, however, the interviewer rather than the respondent writes in the answers to questions. Enough room should be left after each open-ended question to allow writing in the full response. And, though it may seem obvious, interviewers should be equipped with pens that write. The rapport of many an interview has been destroyed by an interviewer frantically rummaging for another pen.

The interview schedule should move from the general to the specific. This is called a *funnel approach*. It begins with general, nonthreatening, orienting questions and gradually leads to more detailed ones. In addition, specific instructions to the interviewer may be included for rephrasing of questions that are not receiving clear, complete, or relevant responses. This attempt to standardize the interviewer's language increases the chances that the information gathered from different respondents will be comparable. If more than one interviewer is used, interviewers should be trained through direct instruction and through role playing techniques so that their interviewing behavior is similar. Whenever possible, the questions asked of different respondents should be identical or similar enough to make sure that respondents are interpreting the meanings of the questions in the same way.

Sometimes, during the course of an interview, respondents may give vague, partial, circular, or irrelevant responses. A technique for encouraging respondents to clarify their responses is *probing*. Probing is "continued neutral questioning" that has the purpose of either clarifying responses or redirecting the respondent to answer a question more precisely. Some examples of common interviewer's probes are "In what way?," "Could you explain that in more detail?," "What do you mean by that?" Or, a simple reflective probe might be used. Here the interviewer repeats the respondent's last few words or a key phrase from a preceding response in a questioning manner. The respondent is thereby encouraged to expand on his previous response.

The interview concludes with the interviewer briefly summarizing how he plans to use the information and offering the respondent an opportunity to make any additional comments about issues covered or neglected by the questionnaire. Since future contact with the respondent may be required, it is important that positive rapport be maintained throughout the interview and that the respondent feel that his contribution is appreciated.

4. Pretesting the Interview Schedule

As does the questionnaire, the interview schedule requires pretesting, ideally with a subsample of the population for which it is intended. Issues of time, ambiguity of questions, logical flow of the interview, uncovered but relevant topics, and the like are dealt with in this manner.

5. Administering the Interview

When the interview is ready to be conducted, one must consider ways in which to encourage complete responses. The chances of this happening are greatest when the interview is conducted in a private setting where there are few distractions. When arranging for an interview, particularly with busy people like agency administrators, it is helpful to indicate to them in advance the amount of time necessary for the interview. In this way the administrator can set aside a block of time in which hopefully there will be few interruptions.

6. Editing, Collating, and Coding the Responses

Immediately after the interview, the interviewer should record information that he did not previously record. In addition, he should edit those responses he did record so that they are legible and coherent.

When all the interviews are completed, information should be collated from the various interviews. This may require the "coding" or categorization of open-ended responses. What this means is developing a response system *after* the information has been gathered. Although the sequence is different from that in questionnaire construction, the same rules apply for developing response categories. Categories should be mutually exclusive and exhaustive. By coding open-ended responses one can go beyond simply comparing qualitative answers to actually counting the numbers or percentages of respondents giving a certain type of response to a particular question.

Hypothetical Illustration

PROBLEM SITUATION AND ADMINISTRATIVE TASK

A director of a community center that serves adolescents is concerned about the fact that many of the youngsters who participate in the program are taking drugs of various kinds. He wants to know about existing or anticipated services for adolescent drug abusers in the local community. Beyond this, he is contemplating planning a drug counseling program in his own agency and would benefit from a knowledge of existing programs and their success or failure in dealing with teenage drug abuse.

There are several decisions that he might make in the future depending upon his knowledge of available resources in the community. He might consider expanding his program to include drug counseling if there is sufficient need and insufficient available resources and if he can obtain the financing and staff to develop such a program. Or, he might develop an information and referral service within the center to refer youngsters with drug-related problems to existing programs in the local community. He might discover that the teenagers he is most concerned about are already receiving services from these agencies and that there is no need for additional service of any kind.

PREPARING FOR, DESIGNING, AND PRETESTING THE INTERVIEW SCHEDULE

1. The Purpose of the Interview

Once the general problem has been identified, the purpose of the interview must be specified. In this illustration, the purpose is to locate agencies that are offering programs for teenagers with drug problems. In addition, one would want to know in detail the kinds of services offered, eligibility criteria, demand for service, degree of success or failure in the program, and so on.

2. Information to Be Gathered

Once the purpose has been specified, one begins by seeking available information about existing programs. Some cities have directories of social service agencies that include information about existing programs. Planning and coordinating councils, as well, frequently have this kind of information readily available. There may also be referral services or telephone "hotlines" that keep lists of services available to community residents. From these, a preliminary list of potentially relevant agencies and program administrators is compiled. Information about additional programs may be secured from knowledgeable respondents in interviews.

Content areas to be covered in the interview are then listed. In this case, the areas considered most important are: the goals of agency programs dealing with teenage drug abuse; the services offered in these programs; degree of client utilization of these services; agency plans for expanding, contracting, or otherwise changing existing services; knowledge of relevant service programs elsewhere in the community.

3. Conducting the Interview

After content areas and agencies to be contacted have been identified, an interview schedule is developed. The interview schedule is pretested, and then program administrators in relevant agencies are contacted, informed of the purpose of the interview, and asked if they would set aside an hour for this purpose. In addition, administrators are asked to provide any available written material about relevant programs, services provided, utilization statistics, and so forth.

In the interviews themselves, the interviewer should be sensitive to the possibility that his agency might be perceived as a threat to existing agencies, particularly if his agency is planning competing service programs. The focus of the interview therefore should be on possibilities for program coordination. Attention is given to possible gaps in available services or in service coordination. This information can serve as a basis for future program planning. Overall, the interviewer should probe for as much specific factual information as possible, taking care to maintain a neutral, noncritical stance.

An interview with an agency executive might go something like this:

INTERVIEWER: "Can you tell me something about the services your agency provides?"

RESPONDENT: "Yes, we provide services that range from family counseling to homemaker services to groupwork. You name it, we've got it."

INTERVIEWER: "Well, specifically what sorts of programs do you have for serving adolescents?"

RESPONDENT: "Probably, we are most likely to see adolescents in our family counseling programs."

INTERVIEWER: "Could you estimate what proportion of family counseling cases involve problems with adolescents?"

RESPONDENT: "I'm not sure, but I can give you our latest summary statistics. I think it's about 20 percent."

INTERVIEWER: "I'd appreciate those statistics. Offhand, would you say that many of these cases involve drug problems?"

RESPONDENT: "That's hard to say. We're generally so busy that I rarely have time to look at the specifics of these cases. We do employ a consulting psychologist to deal with problems related to substance abuse but we do not have a program specifically designed to meet this problem. I suppose we should."

INTERVIEWER: "Why do you say that?"

RESPONDENT: "Well drugs are an increasing problem in this neighborhood, yet we have no program to directly deal with it. There is, however, a new program on the other side of town that is starting a drug counseling service. Perhaps you should see them. I'd be happy to give you their address.''

INTERVIEWER: ''That's very kind of you. I know how you feel. Our agency is also experiencing an increasing incidence of drug use among adolescents. And we're considering introducing a drug prevention program. Do you have any suggestions? . . .''

The foregoing excerpt illustrates asking questions that move from the general to the specific, attempting to be sensitive to the needs and problems of the respondent, and being attentive to the possibilities of locating new sources of information and potential service.

4. Editing, Collating, and Coding the Responses

After each interview, the responses are edited and continuously collated for new sources of information, refinement of questions, and so on. After all the interviews are conducted, agencies may be categorized by the kinds of services offered, numbers served, estimates of success or failure, and so on. This information could serve as the basis for a report on existing community services as well as establishing the need for additional services.

EXERCISE

In your community locate agencies or organizations serving the physically handicapped. From a list of these agencies, select five and arrange to interview program administrators in each.

Devise an interview schedule for determining the range of services offered by these agencies, eligibility requirements, fees, utilization, and judgments about success or failure in meeting community need in this area.

Pretest the interview schedule and conduct the interviews. Collate the information and develop categories for describing the services offered as well as those needed in the community and not offered.

SELECTED BIBLIOGRAPHY

Fear, Richard A. *The Evaluation Interview*. New York: McGraw-Hill, 1973.
Kadushin, Alfred. *The Social Work Interview*. New York: Columbia University Press, 1972.

Kahn, Robert L., and Charles F. Cannell. *The Dynamics of Interviewing*. New York: John Wiley and Sons, 1965.

Merton, Robert K., and Patricia L. Kendall. "The Focused Interview," *American Journal of Sociology*, 51 (1946), 541–57.

Rossi, Peter H. *A Brush-up on Interviewing Technique*. Chicago: National Opinion Research Center, University of Chicago, 1962.

CHAPTER FOUR

Assessing Research in Planning Intervention Strategies

THE ASSESSMENT OF RESEARCH is a skill that is increasingly demanded of program planners and administrators. This activity involves reading, interpreting, and evaluating information from empirical studies. Research reports may take the form of published studies in books and professional journals, unpublished studies conducted by other social agencies, or "in house" studies conducted within an agency itself.

Typically, research studies follow the same basic format: a section devoted to the *formulation of the problem* for research, which includes the questions and hypotheses posed for the study, the assumptions and setting of the study, the relation of the research problem to available knowledge; a section devoted to the *methodology* of the study, which includes the design of the research, sampling considerations, types of data collected, the validity and reliability of the procedures for data collection; and a section devoted to *data analysis and conclusions,* which includes the manipulation, description, and interpretation of the data, conclusions regarding the questions or hypotheses posed, and discussion of the implications of the findings for future research and/or practice.

ASSESSING RESEARCH IN SOCIAL PROGRAM ADMINISTRATION

The ability to critically assess research is useful in all aspects of program planning and administration. A program planner, for example, should be able to evaluate intelligently the kinds of need surveys and resource surveys discussed in the preceding chapters. Through so doing, he can make informed decisions about planning new programs that are nonredundant and relevant to community needs. In program monitoring, an administrator should be able to read the results of a "time and motion" study to determine whether organizational units or individuals are less productive or efficient than they should be. Finally, if evaluation research is to serve practice, it must be read and understood by those administrators and program planners who have ultimate responsibility for translating research findings into policy recommendations.

In this chapter, we focus on the appraisal of research literature for the selection of intervention strategies. The term *intervention strategies* refers to the techniques and procedures that might be employed by staff in social programs of various kinds. In mental hospitals, for example, staff may employ behavioral modification procedures, chemotherapy, Rogerian therapy, transactional analysis. In schools, traditional teaching, teaching machines, and peer tutorials are among the intervention strategies employed.

Although we recognize that the choice of intervention is affected by many different factors—for example, funding opportunities, agency traditions, staff competencies, and community values and norms—our purpose is to maximize the use of available empirical findings in the decision making process. This kind of organizational rationality is extremely important because the decisions on intervention have implications for the type of staff required to implement a new program, the material resources required, training needs for existing staff, and so on. Moreover, the choice of intervention will determine how well and at what cost the clientele of the agency will be served. Thus, it is vital that program planners know which techniques are available to deal with a given problem, what evidence there is of their relative effectiveness and efficiency, and what would be the organizational consequences of their implementation. Such information would also be helpful in evaluating the intervention strategy that is ultimately adopted by the program.

LOCATING RELEVANT RESEARCH

Where do planners find relevant research reports? First, research reports are frequently available from agencies or programs employing technologies that are of interest to the planner. Second, relevant research may be located in the professional literature devoted to the problems to which a program addresses itself. So, for example, the search for reports on different interventions with juvenile delinquents may begin with the *Journal of Crime and Delinquency, Probation, Journal of Alcoholism and Drug Abuse,* and so on. Third, there are guides to the research literature that cite studies by subject or by the key concepts with which they are concerned—for example, *The Reader's Guide to Periodical Literature, Psychological Abstracts, Social Work Abstracts, Poverty and Human Resources Abstracts, Sociological Abstracts.* Finally, the subject index of the card catalogue of a good research library can be used to locate relevant books and research monographs.

PRINCIPLES FOR ASSESSING RESEARCH REPORTS

1. Getting an Overview of the Report

Before reading a research report in depth, one should first read through it quickly to get an overview of the material presented in the report and to determine whether the study deals with relevant intervention strategies in sufficient depth to warrant a more detailed analysis.

2. Operationalizing the Intervention Strategy

After getting an overview of the study, one should then determine the extent to which the report operationalizes the intervention strategies employed. By this we mean whether the study describes intervention strategies in terms that are clear, identifiable, and reproducible in the setting in which the program planner functions. Of course, in a journal article, space limitations may prevent detailed operationalization. In that case, the reader should determine whether a full description of the intervention technique employed is available either in other references cited in the study or directly from the researcher. A full operationalization would not only describe the technique itself but would include information about who employs the technique, the training and skills required to use it, the characteristics of the clientele, and the agency context in which the technique was implemented.

3. Criteria of Effectiveness and Efficiency

Once the intervention strategies have been clearly identified, one should then determine the criteria used in assessing the effectiveness and efficiency of the techniques employed. For example, a teaching machine may be used to teach first-grade students addition and subtraction through programmed instruction. To what extent does the study provide information about the effectiveness of this technique as compared with more traditional teaching methods, tutorial sessions, and so on? To what extent does it provide information about the cost of achieving this level of effectiveness? Finally, how does the efficiency of this method, that is, the relationship between effectiveness and cost, compare with the efficiency of other intervention strategies?

4. Determining the Level of Knowledge Sought in the Research Report

There are three levels of knowledge attained by research studies: *descriptive, correlational,* and *cause-effect.* Description is the lowest level of knowledge. A descriptive study simply describes the interventions employed by a program. Correlational studies present a higher level of knowledge. In these studies, the use of particular intervention strategies is statistically correlated with other variables of interest. For example, a correlational study may report on the drop-out rates of various social class or racial groups from a family-life education program.

At the highest level of knowledge are cause-effect studies. These studies would treat the intervention technology as the *independent* or causal variable and attempt to measure its impact on the basis of changes in a *dependent* or outcome variable. For example, a study may report on the impact of desensitization procedures (independent variables) on the reduction of school phobias in children (dependent variable). The reduction of school phobias, then, is attributable in such a study to the intervention technique employed. Moreover, in a cause-effect study other possible explanations for the result are tested and ruled out.

5. Assessing Measurement Accuracy, Reliability, and Validity

Whatever the level of knowledge sought, the quality of a research report depends to a large degree on the accuracy, reliability, and validity of the measures it employs.

Measurement accuracy refers to the degree of freedom from error in the measuring process that is achieved in the study. It concerns itself with whether or not mistakes have been made in the clerical processing and tabulation of the data.

Accuracy also pertains to the achievement of measurement scales with mutually exclusive and exhaustive categories. In social research three kinds of scales are generally used: nominal, ordinal, and interval. *Nominal scales* are the simplest. In these simple scales, data are classified into categories that imply no rank ordering or hierarchy. An example of a nominal scale is the variable of sex, which is classified as male or female but implies no rank ordering. *Ordinal scales* present categories in an order of some kind. Social class is such a variable, with categories such as low, middle, and high. *Interval scales* are similar to ordinal scales except that they are even more refined. They are calibrated so that the units of measurement along the scale are equidistant. An interval scale contains units that are mutually exclusive, exhaustive, and ordered. An interval scale on income with a dollar as the basic unit is so refined that the difference between an income of $110 and $111 is the same as the difference between an income of $130 and $131. In standard texts on statistical methods, the most appropriate statistical measures for correlating these scales are discussed. For example, a phi correlation can be calculated between variables with nominal measurements; a rho rank-order correlation with ordinal measurement; and Pearson's r with interval measurement.

Reliability refers to consistency in response to a given set of measurements and to freedom from bias. Two typical indicators of reliability are *test-retest* reliability and *interobserver* reliability. In the former, if repeated measurements on the same variable—for example, levels of patient anxiety prior to psychotherapy—produce consistent responses, then the measurement is assumed to be reliable. Often this is reported in correlational terms with a correlation of 0.0 representing complete nonreliability, 0.50 moderate reliability, 0.80 high reliability, and 1.00 perfect reliability. In studies in which observers rate a phenomenon—for example, studies in which caseworkers rate the success of casework intervention by looking at case records—interobserver reliability refers to the extent to which different caseworkers will give the same record the same success score. Measures of interobserver reliability are often expressed in correlational terms (as above) or in terms of percentage agreement. When the latter is used, 70 percent agreement or more indicates a reasonably high degree of interobserver reliability.

Validity refers to the extent to which a measure measures what it is supposed to be measuring. Pragmatically, it means the measurement device is directly relevant to the concept being measured. This is called *content validity*. *Predictive validity* refers to whether the measure predicts other phenomena that are assumed to be associated with the variable. For example, if we were using an attitude questionnaire to measure community involvement, the content validity of the items would refer to whether they measure what we generally mean when we use the term "community involvement." An agree/disagree item such as "I feel very much a part of the community in which I live" would have high content validity. An item such as "I like to work near to where I live" would not. To measure predictive validity, one would see how these measures of attitudinal involvement in the community correlate with actual attendance at city council meetings, community activities, and the like.

In assessing a research report, the reader should determine whether sufficient evidence of the accuracy, reliability, and validity of measures is presented. One would have little confidence in a conclusion that "clients who received therapy were significantly less anxious" if the measure of anxiety was not accurate, reliable, and valid.

6. Assessing the Relationship between Intervention and Outcome

Next one should assess the strength, direction, and predictability of the relationship between the intervention strategy and the results obtained. The *strength of the relationship* is determined by the degree of association between the intervention strategy and the desired outcome. It may be expressed in percentage differences, mean differences, or correlation coefficients. A study that employs percentage differences would indicate the strength of the relationship through one or more of the following comparisons: the percentage difference in a desired outcome between those who received the intervention and a matched group that received no intervention (that is, control group); the percentage difference in a desired outcome between groups that received different interventions (that is, contrast groups;) the percentage difference in a desired outcome within a group before and after receiving the intervention (that is, a group serving as its own control); the percentage difference on a desired outcome between a group that received an authentic intervention and a group that received a placebo intervention.

On outcome measures that are expressed in numerical scores—for example, reading grade level, I.Q., anxiety level—comparisons may be made by showing the differences in the arithmetic averages or mean scores on a desired outcome between the group that received the intervention and any of the comparison groups mentioned above.

The strength of the relationship between intervention and outcome may also be expressed in the form of a correlation coefficient. As we stated earlier, most correlation coefficients can vary in strength from 0.0 to 1.0. However, in assessing the strength of a relationship between intervention and outcome, one would not ordinarily expect correlations as high as one would for a test of reliability. A correlation of approximately .25 would be considered strong enough to justify the generalization that an intervention had some association with the desired outcome. A correlation of .50 would be considered substantial and a correlation of .70 would be considered very high.

Some correlation coefficients (for example, Pearson's *r,* Spearman's rho) are expressed in positive or negative terms. These measures range from −1.00 to +1.00 and indicate the *direction* as well as the strength of the relationship between variables. A negative correlation would indicate an *inverse* relationship between variables—that is, as one variable increases the other decreases. A positive correlation would indicate a *direct* relationship. Thus if an intervention were designed to reduce feelings of powerlessness, one would hope for a strong inverse correlation between intervention and outcome. On the other hand, if an intervention was designed to increase assertiveness, one would hope for a strong direct correlation.

One advantage of correlation coefficients, as compared with percentage and mean difference data, is that with a correlation coefficient it is possible to approximate the predictability of a given outcome when one knows the correlation between intervention and outcome. *Predictability* refers to the percentage of the variation on the outcome variable that can be explained by the intervention. By squaring the correlation coefficient and multiplying by 100 one gets an approximation of predictability. So, for example, if a study concluded that there was a correlation of .50 between participation in a peer tutorial program and improved reading scores, by squaring the correlation coefficient and multiplying by 100 one would predict that approximately 25 percent of the change in reading scores was accounted for by participation in the tutorial program.

7. Assessing Empirical Generality

Empirical generality refers to whether the findings of a study can be generalized to other comparable situations and to other populations of clients and practitioners. The use of random sampling techniques (to be discussed in the chapter on sampling) increases the likelihood that findings can be generalized by making possible the computation of measures of statistical significance of the relationship between intervention and outcome. *Statistical significance* refers to whether the relationship between intervention and outcome found in the population studied reflects a true relationship in the population to which one would like to generalize, or is simply a product of chance fluctuations. Assuming that the study population was randomly selected, on the basis of the laws of probability one can calculate statistical significance by means of various measures of association between intervention and outcome, for example, chi-square, t-tests, correlation coefficients. Social scientists have generally accepted findings that are significant at the .05 level or lower (.01, .001) as indicative of a statistically significant relationship. This means that the findings of the study were such that given the size of the study population, they could have occurred only 5 times in 100 by chance alone.

Measures of statistical significance, however, can be misleading because of the manner in which they are calculated. The larger the study population is, the weaker the relationship between intervention and outcome need be to be judged statistically significant. For example, in a study with a sample population of 100, a 35 percent change on an outcome measure may be required to attain statistical significance. In a similar study with a sample population of 1,000 a change of only 3 percent on the outcome measure may be required. In other words, with a large enough study population a weak relationship may still be statistically significant. Consequently, measures of statistical significance tell us more about whether we can generalize from the sample to the population it represents than they tell us about the strength of a relationship between intervention and outcome.

Another way of assessing the level of empiricial generality is to determine whether the findings of the study have been replicated elsewhere in other studies. If one is able to locate comparable studies and they yield findings of similar strength and direction one can have greater confidence in the knowledge one has concerning the results of a given intervention.

Finally, in making decisions about the possible adoption of intervention strategies discussed in a study or a group of studies, one should consider the extent to which the characteristics of practitioners, clientele, and setting match those in one's own agency or practice context.

8. Assessing Internal Control

In order to establish that a cause-effect relationship exists between the intervention strategy and a desired outcome, one must rule out alternative possible explanations for the outcome. This is accomplished through internal *control* procedures.

There are several questions one should ask to assess the adequacy of internal controls in a study. First, are changes observed directly traceable to the intervention? Second, is there evidence that the changes followed rather than preceded the intervention? Third, is there evidence that changes are not simply the result of growth or maturity or other external factors influencing the research subjects? Fourth, is it clear that observed positive changes are not a consequence of a desire for positive outcomes on the part of the researcher? In other words, are the measures of success fair and unbiased? Fifth, is there evidence that observed changes are not a result of the respondents' desires to please the researcher, that is, what is generally referred to as the "Hawthorne effect"? And finally, is there evidence that observed changes are the result of an authentic intervention rather than a response to a falsely perceived intervention, that is, "placebo effect"?

Many of these questions are dealt with in research studies through the use of control groups and the use of statistical procedures to test for alternative explanations. By limiting the subject population to single categories of individuals—for example, females, blacks, or middle-income clients—one can rule out the confounding effects of sex, race, or social class on a given outcome.

9. Assessing Possibilities of Implementation

The criteria discussed in the foregoing sections can be used to assess the general quality of a research study. However, when considering the possible adoption of an intervention strategy in one's own agency or program, one should ask the following questions:

a. Is the technology discussed relevant to my program? How does it compare with other technologies available?

b. What would be the relative cost of employing the technology in my program? How does this compare with other technologies available?

c. What staff and training needs would be required if the technology were to be adopted? Would new staff have to be hired? Would existing staff have to be retrained? How does this compare with other technologies available?

d. Does the technology have to be further specified to make it operational in my agency?

e. How effective and efficient is the technology in comparison with other technologies available?

The answers to these questions should then be weighed against the quality of evidence presented in the research report. Next, similar questions should be asked concerning the technologies currently employed by the agency. What is the quality of evidence offered concerning the effectiveness and efficiency of the intervention strategies currently employed? In this way more rational decision making concerning intervention strategies can be achieved.

HYPOTHETICAL ILLUSTRATION

PROBLEM SITUATION AND ADMINISTRATIVE TASK

An educational administrator wants to reduce disruptive behaviors and to increase behaviors conducive to learning in junior high schools. He is considering two possible programs. Approach A would enlist a special education staff to work with the disruptive youths in the classrooms. Approach B would be to use social work staff to work with disruptive youths and their families outside the schools. Natually, it would be important for the administrator to have information about the relative efficiency and effectiveness of each of the proposed alternatives.

CONSULTING THE RESEARCH LITERATURE

Through the reference library at a local university, the administrator is able to locate a number of studies dealing with the management of disruptive classroom behavior. Since there is a considerable literature on this topic, he confines his attention to studies that go beyond simple description of program and attempt to measure the outcomes of various intervention strategies. Moreover, he narrows his focus to studies that deal with adolescents and that involve strategies A or B.

1. Getting an Overview

First, the studies are read quickly to determine whether they fully describe intervention strategies as well as the roles of the staff who implement them, students, teachers, and parents. In addition, one would want to know whether the studies clearly describe measures of success or failure. If at first reading these crucial data are present, it would appear that a more thorough assessment of the study is warranted.

2. Operationalizing the Intervention Strategy

In those studies that are relevant it becomes apparent that descriptions of behavioral modification techniques used in classroom interventions are more complete than descriptions of the interventions used with parents. Given the fact that strategy B involves work with parents as well as students and teachers, it is clear that strategy B would be more costly in time and effort. This would not automatically lead to its rejection, however, since questions of effectiveness should be considered before such a judgment is made.

3. Criteria of Effectiveness and Efficiency

A next step is to assess the measurement of effectiveness of intervention techniques. In some studies of technique a very limited number of behavioral measures was used to indicate only the reduction in disruptive behaviors. Other studies indicated not only the reduction in disruptive behaviors but changes in grade-point averages, reading scores, and so on. The studies devoted to strategy B employed more diffuse measures of parental satisfaction with the program. Comments made by parents suggested that rather than being measures of effectiveness they were more like statements of gratitude for staff efforts in behalf of their children. There are no direct data presented on the efficiency of the two approaches.

4. Level of Knowledge Sought

All the studies located either imply or assert cause-effect relationships between the intervention strategy and the outcome sought. However, only a few of the studies actually test for other possible explanations for the findings.

5. Assessing Measurement Accuracy, Reliability, and Validity

In those studies that involved behavioral modification procedures in the classroom, highly reliable measures of the reduction in disruptive behaviors were developed, based on the use of two or more independent observers in the classrooms. High reliability was indicated by an 80–90 percent agreement on classroom behavior scores. In studies in which classroom behavior scores were supplemented by measures of educational achievement such as grades, reading scores, and the like, measures of school performance were considered most valid. Finally, in those studies devoted to social work intervention with parents, no measures of reliability were offered, and, for the reasons indicated earlier, the validity of the measure of effectiveness was questionable.

6. Assessing the Relationship Between Intervention and Outcome

Studies on behavioral modification procedures reported correlations ranging from $-.21$ to $-.46$ between the intervention and disruptive behaviors. Moreover, in one study a mean difference of 1.3 years on reading scores was reported after 6 months of intervention. In another such study, a 37 percent increase in attendance was reported over the course of a year.

In studies devoted to social work intervention with parents, no comparative data were presented. They did report, however, a high level of parent satisfaction with the program (65 percent) and presented a number of quotations from interviews with parents attesting to the efficacy of the program.

7. Assessing Empirical Generality

None of the studies located employed sampling procedures. All were, in effect, case illustrations or demonstrations of individual projects in individual schools. Consequently, the amount of generalization possible was limited. However, if the degree to which findings were consistent in the various studies is considered and if the populations in the studies are matched as much as possible with those in the administrator's schools, some generalization is possible.

8. Assessing Internal Control

None of the studies found employed control groups for comparison with groups receiving an intervention. Some of the behavioral modification studies, however, reported classroom behavior scores and other school performance scores *prior* to the introduction of the intervention programs. Moreover, most of these studies reported positive change in student *behaviors,* as compared with the studies of casework intervention with parents, which only offered *attitudinal* data. The consistency of the findings, the types of measures of effectiveness employed, and the relative efficiency of the techniques involved all suggest that strategy A, the classroom program, is the preferred strategy.

9. Assessing Possibilities of Implementation

Having determined which strategy makes most sense on the basis of the available empirical evidence, the administrator should then consider the possibilities of implementing this strategy in school settings. After approaching personnel in his schools, however, he learns that the staff in the schools differ in their willingness to employ behavioral approaches in the classroom. Since there is some positive evidence for both approaches and since the effectiveness of the behavior program is not certain, he decides to implement the two different intervention approaches in different schools. On the basis of what he has learned from the literature, he develops comparable measures to evaluate the effectiveness and efficiency of the two approaches in the different school settings.

EXERCISE

1. Select a public health problem—for example, obesity, smoking, alcohol abuse—and locate two studies describing different treatment programs that deal with this problem.

2. Describe fully the interventions used and determine the degree to which the evidence in the two studies supports claims for effectiveness.

3. Now consider the relative efficiency of the two intervention strategies. If there is not sufficient information to determine this, specify the kinds of data required to do so.

SELECTED BIBLIOGRAPHY

Goldstein, Harris K. *Research Standards and Methods for Social Workers.* New Orleans, La.: The Hauser Press, 1963; pp. 299–319.

Isaac, Stephen, with William B. Michael. *Handbook in Research and Evaluation.* San Diego, Cal.: Robert R. Knapp, 1971; pp. 154–61.

Tripodi, Tony. *Uses and Abuses of Social Research in Social Work.* New York: Columbia University Press, 1974; pp. 43–73, 89–106.

Tripodi, Tony, Phillip, Fellin, and Henry J. Meyer. *The Assessment of Social Research.* Itasca, Ill.: F. E. Peacock, 1969; pp. 60–93, 108–30.

CHAPTER FIVE

Using Observational Techniques for Planning Staff Training Programs

DIRECT OBSERVATION is probably the most natural method of gathering information. All of us observe phenomena continually and make decisions based upon our observations. When used for research purposes, however, observation is conducted more systematically and with greater precision than in daily life.

In its most structured form, *systematic observation* is a method of data collection that includes one or more observers observing events or behaviors as they occur and reliably recording their observations in terms of previously structured and validated categories. In some studies, the events or behaviors to be observed are preserved on film, videotape, or audiotape recordings. When situations cannot be observed directly or recorded, they may be rendered in a role play of the event by past participants. Whatever the form of data employed, systematic observation is sufficiently structured to be usable in *testing* research hypotheses.

At the other end of the continuum, unstructured or *nonsystematic observation* involves the observer's writing narrative accounts of his impressions of what he is observing without employing previously structured categories for describing the events or behaviors. Nonsystematic observation is used mainly for descriptive purposes and for *generating* research hypotheses. These hypotheses can then be tested in more systematic ways.

Depending on his relationship to the persons or events observed, the observation researcher may engage in either participant or nonparticipant observation. In *nonparticipant observation*, the researcher does not actively participate in the situation or interact with the subjects of his observation. He remains a passive observer. In *participant observation*, on the other hand, the observer is an active participant in the situation that he observes, and while he tries to not influence the course of the events observed, he interacts freely with the subjects of his observation.

Observation researchers may also be passing or nonpassing observers. A *passing observer* is one who does not reveal his research role to those he is observing. It is frequently assumed that as a result, the behaviors observed will be more spontaneous, responses to questions more candid, and so on. *Nonpassing observers* reveal their research role. In some situations, this strategy results in access to a greater range of informational sources.

Observational techniques are frequently employed when other, more obtrusive techniques, such as questionnaires or interviews, are not appropriate. For example, in situations in which participants are biased, unable to recall events, uninterested, or untrained in the concepts or dynamics with which the observer is concerned, observational techniques are most useful. Through these techniques, information can be gathered about a phenomenon as it occurs, within the conceptual framework of the researcher. In some studies, the observations are followed up and validated by questionnaires, interviews, or more structured observation.

OBSERVATIONAL RESEARCH FOR SOCIAL PROGRAM ADMINISTRATION

Observational research concepts and techniques are useful in all aspects of social program planning and administration. In program planning, for instance, groups of potential clients can be observed in their natural settings—family, work, community, recreation—as a way of diagnosing individual, group, or community problems and planning the kinds of program interventions required. Supervisors can employ observational techniques to monitor the performance of line staff. This monitoring may involve direct observation or the use of tape recordings or role plays. Finally, observational research may be used as a means of evaluating the impact of program interventions. For example, in a residential treatment setting for disturbed children, one can observe the extent to which program interventions have improved the quality of social interaction among the children.

In this chapter, we focus on the use of observational research techniques for program planning. Our case illustration involves a staff training officer's use of observational techniques for planning a staff training program for new workers.

OBSERVATIONAL RESEARCH PRINCIPLES

1. The Purpose of the Observations

It is impossible to observe everything in a family, organization, or community. Consequently, one should decide on the purpose of the observation before considering units and techniques of observation. In social research, decisions on purpose are frequently made in an initial phase in which unsystematic, participant observation takes place. In this way, interesting questions and hypotheses are raised that are then answered through more systematic observation.

In social agencies, administrators and planners generally do not have sufficient free time available to them to use unstructured participant observation to its fullest advantage. However, in the course of their daily activities, they may observe situations, events, or crises that suggest problems and hypotheses for more systematic observation. Thus, an administrator may notice an unusual number of clients angrily leaving intake interviews, slamming doors and looking disgruntled. On this basis, a decision might be made to observe more closely the intake staff and their processing of clientele. The idea for observational research may come as well from outside funding sources. In the quest for greater accountability, observational techniques may be used to determine whether staff are complying with organizational procedures and legal codes. Whatever the impetus for the study, one should first decide on its purpose.

2. What Is to Be Observed?

In order to observe a phenomenon reliably, one must decide upon the behaviors to include and those to exclude from the observations. In addition, one should develop mutually exclusive and exhaustive categories for characterizing the different types of behaviors to be observed. This is facilitated by making a checklist of behaviors to be observed and, in more systematic observation, of the categories for recording these behaviors.

In studying the classroom behaviors of teacher's aides, for example, one may observe the number of verbal interactions initiated by the aides, whether statements are critical, supportive, or primarily informational, whether students initiate interactions with the aides, and so on. Since an infinite number of behaviors can be observed and classified, decisions also have to be made about the behaviors to exclude. Thus, the purpose of the study may make it possible to exclude teacher–teacher's aide interactions, or relationships among teacher's aides, and so on.

The list of behaviors to be observed should generally be limited to those behaviors for which there are clear management or professional expectations and which are subject to change through staff-training efforts. In particular, knowledge, attitudes, and skills of staff that are expected by the agency can serve as a frame of reference for choosing the categories of observation.

Suppose a public health program hires paraprofessionals to make primary contacts with potential clientele, to provide them with knowledge about the health program, and to assist them in identifying health problems that can be treated within the program. It is expected that, in contacts with community residents, the paraprofessionals be able to *listen* to what a potential client says and not dismiss his concerns, and to *focus* the discussion on problems that are health related and for which the program provides services. In addition, the paraprofessional is expected to have *knowledge of community resources* to which he can refer a person for services not offered by the health program itself. Hence, a list of general areas for observation would include interviewing skills, knowledge of community resources, and referrals based on this knowledge. If it were established that staff performance was deficient in any of these areas, training programs could be devised to correct the deficiencies.

Earlier we said that the categories within these areas of observation should be mutually exclusive and exhaustive. More specifically, let us consider the area of knowledge of community resources. At the simplest level, the area could be divided into three categories: has adequate knowledge, does not have adequate knowledge, insufficient information to make a judgment. Or observations could be put into a more complex rating scale on which varying degrees of knowledge are indicated. In general, the most reliable types of observations are made where the observer or observers have fewest discriminations to make. However, for some purposes more complex discriminations are necessary.

A final consideration in devising categories is the *level of inference* required by the observer. In general, the closer the inference is to the actual manifest content of the observation, the more reliable the observation will be. In the preceding example, it would be more reliable to determine ''knowledge of community resources'' on the basis of a checklist of specific agencies mentioned than through a more subjective judgment of adequacy of knowledge. Or, in the teacher's aide example, it would be more reliable to count the number of times an aide shouts at children in a specified period of time than to make more global judgments about whether the aide is or isn't hostile. In other words, the more behaviorally specific the observation, the greater the likelihood of agreement among independent observers of a set of events.

3. Site and Medium of Observation

Observational research requires that the site for the observations be standardized. In observing patient behavior in a mental hospital, one would observe them at specified times and places in their day. In observing group-workers at work, one might confine oneself to observations of interactions with groups that have just begun, or groups that have been meeting for more than two months. This kind of standardization is necessary for valid comparisons of the subjects of observation.

In addition, it is important to specify what medium or media of observation are to be used, since direct observation is not always possible. If videotape recordings are to be used as the source of data, equipment and tapes must be available, subjects must agree to the procedure, and staff must be technically competent to use the equipment.

When neither direct observation nor recording of an event is possible, role playing of critical incidents can be a useful device for recreating specific situations. In such role plays, staff may perform the roles of themselves as well as of clients. While this technique is not as good as direct observation, it often suggests typical problem situations and client or worker responses to them. Moreover, role plays can be used both to identify training needs and as a vehicle for training.

4. Information Units

Once the observer has identified the areas and categories of observation, he must decide what his unit of information for categorization should be. The more systematic the observation, the more standardized the unit of information must be. In an interview situation, a unit of information may be anything from each word in the interview to each sentence to whole sections of the interview. In a group situation, the unit of information for analysis may be the number of times a particular event occurs. In an agency, it may refer to the presence or absence of a phenomenon, service, or facility.

Naturally, the more detailed the observation and the smaller the unit of information, the more time-consuming and costly the observational research will be. It would take much more time to code a tape-recorded interview on the basis of word units than it would to code on the basis of whole sections of the interview. Therefore, the unit of information should be small enough so that it provides reliable and valid information pertinent to the purpose of observation but not so small that it requires excessive amounts of time for coding.

5. Frequency of Observations

In most situations, for reasons of economy, observations must be made on a selective basis. For example, it might be important but prohibitively expensive to observe nursing staff all day, every day, for a month. Hence it is frequently necessary to select a time sample. A *time sample* involves making observations at previously designated periods of time to obtain what is hopefully a representation of typical observee behavior. The times for observation may be selected randomly (see chapter on sampling) or systematically, or they may be based on some strategic sense of the most critical aspects of the observed phenomenon. Thus, nursing staff may be observed five times a day at randomly selected times. Or, they may be observed five times a day at one-hour intervals. Another mode of sampling would be more purposive and based on a knowledge of the times when the most critical aspects of nursing staff performance might be observed, for example, during ward rounds, administration of medication, assistance to the doctors, and so on.

As much as possible, the time sample selected should reflect typical staff behaviors. Moreover, if staff are to be compared they should be observed during comparable time or functional periods. This will increase the reliability of the observational system and of the generalizations that can be made.

6. Who Does the Observing?

In most situations the decision about who does the observing is not a difficult one. It is important, however, that the observer have a familiarity with the situation he is observing. This is particularly important if the coding system requires that he make inferences from the information available to him. Consequently, only a person skilled and experienced in interviewing should make judgments about another's interviewing skills. If the observational scheme does not require such inferences, a high degree of familiarity with the phenomen is not required. Sometimes observational research requires further training for those who are doing the observing.

Observations can be made by trained outsiders as well as by routine participants in a system. In an agency, line workers, supervisors, and administrators may all conduct systematic observation. Whatever his usual role in the situation, the observer should try to refrain from projecting his own biases and values on the behaviors observed. This is often very difficult. However, the best observers are those who can be objective, impartial, open to new information, and free of prejudice about the events and individuals to be observed.

7. Not Influencing the Observation Situation

In attempting to be as objective as possible, the observer avoids influencing those he is observing. As much as possible, his stance should be neutral and he should not intervene in behalf of any of the participants in the situation observed.

Even if he says nothing, however, his mere presence, or the presence of a tape recorder, may significantly affect the behaviors of those observed. Because of this, it is advisable to give participants some time to get used to the presence of the observer or the recording equipment. Real data should not be collected until the observer is relatively confident that the participants in the situation are able to ignore the presence of the observer or the recording equipment.

8. Reliability of Observation

To insure a high degree of reliability in the observations, observers should be trained in the preceding principles and should practice making the desirable observations. When a number of observers are used, training and practice are necessary until a high level of interobserver reliability is achieved. Here, *interobserver reliability* refers to the extent to which two or more independent observers observing the same situation and using the same set of categories agree in their judgments and coding of the event. A simple index of interobserver reliability is a percentage based on the number of agreements between the judges relative to the total number of judgments that they make multiplied by 100. An index of 70–80 percent agreement is generally regarded as fairly high.

For each observer used, a high degree of intraobserver reliability is also desirable. *Intraobserver reliability* refers to the extent to which a single observer repeatedly codes the same events in the same way. With recorded data this is computed relatively easily by rerunning taped events, observing and coding them, and computing a percentage based on the number of agreements in judgments that the individual observer makes, relative to the total number of judgments that he makes, multiplied by 100. Here again a 70–80 percent reliability is generally required.

Finally, one should not assume that once established a high degree of reliability is easily maintained. Observers get tired or bored and their reliability declines. As they become more familiar with the situation to be observed, they become less attentive to new aspects or prejudge the course of events. To protect against these possibilities, spot checking should be done throughout the study. If a high degree of reliability is maintained throughout the study, one can have more confidence in the inferences drawn from the study's findings.

HYPOTHETICAL ILLUSTRATION

PROBLEM SITUATION AND ADMINISTRATIVE TASK

A family service agency receives funding to expand its outreach program for casefinding in a low-income area of the city. The agency currently employs two paraprofessional workers who are considered to be highly successful in doing this kind of work. The additional funding makes possible the hiring of five additional paraprofessionals for this function. The staff training officer in the agency is given the task of hiring the new workers and developing a training program for them.

After initial discussions with the paraprofessionals already on staff, it is determined that they are not sufficiently aware of the techniques they use in their daily work to give the training officer a comprehensive account of the kinds of information, knowledge, and skills required to perform the job. Consequently, a decision is made to observe these workers systematically in order to derive information about what kinds of people would be most suited to the job and about the kind of training they should receive.

PLANNING AND IMPLEMENTING AN OBSERVATIONAL STUDY

1. The Purpose of the Observation

The purpose of this study is to determine the personal characteristics, information, knowledge, and skills that seem to be required for successful performance in casefinding and referral in a low-income area. The findings will be used to screen applicants for the new positions and to train those who are hired.

2. What Is to Be Observed?

The subject of the observational research is the on-the-job functioning of the present paraprofessional staff. More specifically, their techniques for contacting potential clients, informing them about the agency's function, informing them about the functions of other agencies, and following up or making referrals will be observed.

3. Site and Medium of Observation

It is decided that the simplest, least costly, and most valid way for the staff training officer to gather the necessary information is through direct observation of the paraprofessionals in their daily work. An observation form is developed that includes time and place of contact with potential clients, the manner in which the worker introduces himself and explains the agency's function, the way in which the worker explores possible problems of the client, the way in which knowledge about resources available from other agencies is utilized, procedures for referring the person to another agency, procedures for engaging the client in the host agency's program, and so on. In many respects, this form resembles a semistructured interview schedule. However, in this study, the answers to the questions are derived from observation rather than from verbal responses of the individuals observed.

After the initial set of observations is completed, the training officer may wish to verify his initial inferences by interviewing the paraprofessional workers and asking them questions for further clarification, engaging them in role plays of both typical and atypical situations experienced in the field, or following up with more systematic observation. Ultimately, the form developed for observing the staff paraprofessionals may also become useful for training, monitoring, and evaluating the new paraprofessional staff.

4. Information Units

In the initial stages of the study, the information units refer to those aspects of the worker's behaviors that relate to the different functional components of the job. Therefore, the observer does not attempt to code every word or every sentence but codes whole sections of the worker's interaction with potential clients. The form serves as a guide to these sections.

5. Frequency of Observations

Observations will take place on three randomly selected days during a two-week period for each worker. Or, on the basis of greater knowledge of the range of workers' tasks, they may take place on days when different aspects of the workers' job are highlighted. For example, one set of observations may take place on days when workers are engaged in contact with other agencies. Another set of observations may take place when workers are making contact with potential clients. A third set of observations may take place when workers are making follow-up visits with actual clients. Naturally, this last, more refined observational study would require separate observation forms for each aspect of the workers' functioning.

6. Who Does the Observing?

In this example, it is clear that the staff training officer does the observing. However, if a form were developed for monitoring and evaluating the new workers, then the original paraprofessional staff might ultimately be doing the observing.

7. Not Influencing the Observation Situation

During the period of direct field observation it is essential that the staff training officer not influence the situation that he is observing. To this end, he should make the purpose of his observations clear and reassure the paraprofessionals he is observing that he is not evaluating their performance. Indeed, he may enlist the greatest cooperation from the paraprofessionals by highlighting the fact they are being used as prototypes for the training of new workers.

It is equally important that a strategy be worked out to put potential clients at ease about the presence of the observer. This may be particularly difficult in situations in which the paraprofessional worker has an established relationship with a client. Some discussion must therefore take place *before* the field observation about how the observer will be introduced, how his function will be explained, whether he actually takes notes during the observation sessions, and so on.

8. Reliability of the Observation

In the present example, since there is only one observer, intraobserver reliability is a concern. Since observations will not be recorded on tape, there will be no way of assessing reliability. However, the training officer can sharpen his observational skills *prior* to doing field observation by observing a series of taped role plays and checking the reliability of his observations on repeated role plays.

Should the observation forms be used by staff paraprofessionals as a basis for monitoring trainee performance, then efforts should be made to assess and maximize interobserver reliability.

EXERCISE

Employing the above principles for making systematic observations, devise a form for observing participation in a staff meeting in an agency, a city council meeting, or a board of education meeting. Determine who participates how frequently, and what the major themes of their contributions seem to be. Using the same form, have a partner observe the same meeting independently. After you have collected the data, compare your two accounts and make an estimate of the interobserver reliability of your observations. If there is low reliability, discuss the reasons for your disagreements. Then revise, if necessary, your observation form and repeat the observation process at another meeting. Check to see whether interobserver reliability has increased.

SELECTED BIBLIOGRAPHY

Becker, Howard S. "Problems of Inference and Proof in Participant Observation," in D. P. Forcese and S. Richter, eds., *Stages of Social Research: Contemporary Perspectives*. Englewood Cliffs, N.J.: Prentice-Hall, 1970; pp. 205–15.

Best, John W. *Research in Education*. 2d ed. Englewood Cliffs, N.J.: Prentice-Hall, 1970; pp. 181–86.

Liberman, R. P., W. J. Derise, Larry W. King, T. A. Eckman, and D. Wood, "Behavioral Measurement in a Community Mental Health Center," in P. O. Davidson, F. W. Clark, and L. A. Hamerlynch, eds., *Evaluation of Behavioral Programs*. Champaign, Ill.: Research Press, 1974; pp. 103–39.

Maas, Henry S., and Norman A. Polansky. "Collecting Original Data," in Norman A. Polansky, ed., *Social Work Research*. Chicago: University of Chicago Press, 1960; pp. 129–41.

McCall, G. J., and J. L. Simmons, eds. *Issues in Participant Observation*. Reading, Mass.: Addison-Wesley, 1969.

Massie, Joseph L. *Essentials of Management*. 2d ed. Englewood Cliffs, N.J.: Prentice-Hall, 1971; pp. 93–103.

Weissman, Harold. *Overcoming Mismanagement in the Human Service Professions*. San Francisco: Jossey-Bass, 1973; pp. 47–75.

PART TWO

PROGRAM MONITORING

PROGRAM MONITORING is the process by which information about program operations is generated and analyzed. It tells the administrator how well program means are being implemented. More specifically, program monitoring involves an appraisal of the extent to which: (1) the designated target population is being served; (2) the quantity and quality of staff performance are satisfactory and consistent with program goals and technologies; and (3) policies comply with predesignated standards, laws, and regulations imposed on the agency by external funding sources, regulatory agencies, professional bodies, and the like.

Monitoring takes place after the planning objectives have been realized. Once program goals have been specified, target populations identified, technologies chosen, and staff recruited and trained, the monitoring function begins.

Monitoring starts with the delineation of performance standards consistent with the planning objectives. Next it requires the systematic collection of information on performance, based on these standards. When this information has been collected, a judgment is made about the extent to which discrepancies exist between actual performance and program expectancies, and an administrative decision is made as to whether program operations should be fundamentally changed or modified or remain the same.

A secondary use of program monitoring is for public relations and for reporting program activities to sponsors. Indeed, the format of information to be routinely collected about program operations may be determined by requirements of the funding sources. This information may then become the basis for annual reports, public relations literature, and the like.

Program monitoring and the information it generates are also useful in areas in which it is difficult to get *direct* measures of program effectiveness. For example, in the process of evaluating a correctional facility it may be impossible to get direct measures of the success of rehabilitation efforts. However, it would be helpful to know how much time inmates spend per week in rehabilitation programs and how this compares with national norms for similar institutions.

In problem areas in which effective and reliable technologies have been developed, program monitoring may be all that is required to measure program effectiveness. Thus, in evaluating a polio vaccination program, all that would be necessary is knowledge about whether the target population has been reached and whether medically appropriate performance standards have been met by staff. Data on the subsequent incidence of polio would be comforting but is not essential to program evaluation.

ADMINISTRATIVE DECISIONS AND PROGRAM MONITORING

Although program monitoring has many uses, its primary purpose is to enable the administrator to make rational and informed decisions about program operations. If he is following a "management by objectives" approach, in which all aspects of program operations are rigorously specified, he is likely to use monitoring information for making precise corrections in the program. If he uses a less behavioristic management approach, program monitoring is likely to affect broader decisions. The extent to which changes are made in a program will depend as well on the degree of accountability of the program to funding sources, clientele, professional groups, and so on.

Program monitoring generates information affecting the following administrative decisions: whether to reallocate staff to different programs or to different geographical areas within a program; whether to increase or decrease staff efforts in relation to particular program functions such as the recruitment of clientele or public relations; whether to ask for an increase in the operational budget for a particular program from program sponsors or other potential funding sources; whether to modify program objectives; whether more skilled staff is needed; in the face of budget cutbacks, whether existing staff activities in a particular program can be reduced or restructured; whether existing program policies and practices are in compliance with legal requirements; and so on.

The administrator of an agency or program has responsibility for these and many other decisions that bear on the quality and quantity of service delivery to a designated clientele. He must modify and revise programs where necessary; select, train, and supervise staff; devise patterns of staff organization and deployment; manage the fiscal activities of the program with adequate and established accounting and auditing procedures; report to sponsors about program operations and progress; make budget requests on the basis of reliable information about program operations; and so on. In short, the administrator and his staff are responsible for reviewing program operations through monitoring procedures and for making decisions based on systematic, reliable, and valid monitoring information.

RESEARCH TECHNIQUES AND PROGRAM MONITORING

Provided that the administrator is effective in fostering staff cooperation, research concepts and techniques can be usefully employed for securing information relevant to many aspects of program monitoring. Thus, the information generated by concepts and techniques discussed here can contribute to social auditing and cost accounting efforts.

In this section, however, our focus is on concepts and techniques directly applicable to nonfiscal aspects of program monitoring. In chapter 6, for example, we discuss the use of forms for conducting a client census. These forms enable the administrator to assess quantitative information about service delivery to a designated clientele and to compare this information with standards related to program expectancies. In our hypothetical illustration, we use forms to monitor a job placement agency's service statistics.

Forms are also useful in assessing staff performance. Chapter 7 is devoted to the use of forms for monitoring staff activity and use of time. In that chapter, we demonstrate the collection of data on staff time and activity in a rural public health program.

Chapter 8 shows how sampling is applied to program monitoring. More specifically, it illustrates the use of random sampling techniques for assessing the quality of staff performance.

In the final chapter in this section, chapter 9, we discuss techniques and principles of data analysis. These techniques and principles are useful for making inferences about the degree to which program data approximate desired standards. In this regard, we look at the staff composition of a hypothetical agency to see whether it is in compliance with "affirmative action" guidelines.

These research methods will be developed in much greater detail in the following chapters; but they are by no means the only approaches applicable to program monitoring. In fact, the methods discussed in the preceding chapters on questionnaire construction, interviews, research assessment, and the use of observational techniques are applicable to program monitoring as well.

The choice of research procedures depends on the particular context in which a study is to be conducted. The usefulness of the information generated, however, depends to a large degree on the quality of the program planning that preceded it. In other words, information about client and staff characteristics and performance is most useful when it can be compared with planned objectives and with measurable standards.

SELECTED BIBLIOGRAPHY

Drucker, Peter F. *Management: Tasks, Responsibilities, Practices.* New York: Harper and Row, 1973; pp. 430–32.

Freeman, Howard E., and Clarence, C. Sherwood. *Social Research and Social Policy.* Englewood Cliffs, N.J.: Prentice-Hall, 1970; pp. 55–69.

Livingstone, John L., and Sanford C. Gunn, eds. *Accounting for Social Goals.* New York: Harper and Row, 1974; pp. 317–45.

Massie, Joseph L. *Essentials of Management.* 2nd ed. Englewood Cliffs, N.J.: Prentice-Hall, 1971; pp. 82–92.

Terry, George R. *Principles of Management.* 6th ed. Homewood, Ill.: Richard D. Irwin, 1972; pp. 535–82.

Tripodi, Tony, Phillip Fellin, and Irwin Epstein. *Social Program Evaluation.* Itasca, Ill.: F. E. Peacock, 1971; pp. 63–79.

CHAPTER SIX

Using Forms to Conduct a Client Census

FORMS CAN BE the bane of bureaucracy. When designed and used properly, however, they are highly efficient devices for program monitoring and administrative control. Forms can be used for monitoring service delivery to various client groups, staff performance, and program outcomes. And while the use of forms is not generally considered a "research technique," good forms make use of concepts and principles that are basic to all research instruments. Moreover, well-constructed and properly completed forms can provide information that is essential to effective administration.

In this chapter, we show how forms can be used to conduct a client census. Such a census offers a quantitative description of program contacts with clientele and makes possible comparison of this information with standards related to overall program objectives. Here, the monitoring process involves designating a target population, delineating service standards in relation to the target population, the selecting of indicators of program contact with clientele, constructing appropriate forms to record the information, collecting and analyzing the information, and comparing the data with previously planned standards of service delivery. As a result, adjustments can be made in client recruitment and/or service patterns.

THE CLIENT CENSUS FOR SOCIAL
PROGRAM ADMINISTRATION

In recent years, funding sources, professional groups, and disadvantaged client groups have demanded greater accountability from social agencies.

Enlightened administrators have joined with these groups in desiring the delivery and documentation of appropriate services for low-income and minority clientele. For some programs, documentation of services has been the difference between staying in business and closing up shop.

The notion of "appropriate services" is especially germane to groups that have argued for more relevant services for their constituencies. The concept has obvious implications for staff recruitment and training as well. Existing staff may have training inappropriate or inadequate to provide the services required by these constituencies. New staff may have to be hired. Existing staff may require in-service training.

In the context of budgetary constraints, it is even more important that administrators be able to describe program activities in relation to client needs. Cost accountants will be concerned with the cost per client served. Moreover, documentation of client contact may become the basis of requests for additional funds in succeeding budget years. If the data do not support such a request, administrative decisions about termination, reallocation of resources, development of new strategies, or whole new programs must be made. For all of these decisions, a census of clients and the services they receive is invaluable.

PRINCIPLES FOR CONDUCTING A CLIENT CENSUS

1. Designation of the Target Population

The target population is that population to which a program should direct its efforts. Strictly speaking, the target population should be specified during the planning phase of program development. In designating target populations, planners should be as operationally specific as possible. This can be facilitated by specifying precisely those characteristics that are related to program eligibility. Such characteristics may include race, sex, age, socioeconomic status, area of residence, employment status, type of problem presented, source of referral to the program, and officially applied labels or diagnostic categories.

For example, a program may be aimed at "rehabilitating juvenile delinquents." In planning such a program and specifying the target population, the planner should consider the scope and capacity of his program. This may mean a decision to limit services to minority-group youngsters, between the ages of 10 and 16, who were adjudged delinquents by the juvenile court for drug-related offences, and who reside in a particular community. The preceding target population is obviously smaller and more selective than one defined as all youngsters in that city who have been referred to the juvenile courts.

As we stated earlier, the target population and its needs should match the capacity and scope of the program. The extent of client need should be determined prior to program initiation through need-assessment surveys, resource surveys, and so on. Ideally, the program should then be designed and staffed to meet the most pressing needs.

2. Delineation of Program Objectives and Standards of Service

Program objectives should also be delineated as specifically as possible during the planning phase of a program. Thus, for example, a general objective such as "rehabilitation" of a delinquent population should be defined operationally in terms of the absence of subsequent delinquent acts, attendance at and performance in school, appropriate behavior at home, and the like.

Next, program objectives should be defined in relation to the target population and to the proportion of eligible persons in that population that the program is expected to serve. In order to do this *standards* need to be articulated. A standard is an expectation of program effort or performance; it is a type of plan, a unit of measurement established to serve as a criterion of program performance. It is established through newly emerging values and norms, past experience, the experience of other comparable programs, hard data, common sense, and guesswork. Program sponsors may determine that a given proportion of the target population must be served or that a given proportion of clients served by the agency should be from the target population.

A United Fund, for example, may determine that more agency services should be directed toward low-income people. Standards of performance for agencies that receive funding may be based on the notion that agency caseloads should reflect the proportion of low-income people in their local communities. Or a decision might be made to overrepresent low-income people in agency caseloads. Whatever the standard, however, it is operationally specific and expressed in terms of the percentage of agency caseload desired.

The principle of standardization is that it provides predetermined patterns and levels for agency or program performance that aid in planning, contribute to efficiency, and expedite the monitoring process for purposes of administrative control and decision making.

3. Construction of Client Census Forms

In many respects, the principles that apply to the construction of questionnaires and interview schedules are equally applicable to the construction of client census forms. Measures should be operationally specific, valid, and reliable. Categories should be mutually exclusive and exhaustive. Questions should relate to a single category of information about the numbers and types of clients in contact with a program, the types of services requested, and the services received. When monitoring is designed to generate information about programmatic results, data about the consequences of program intervention and the conditions surrounding client termination are also collected. Whatever their specific purpose, client census forms should be constructed with the following principles in mind:

a. The information gathered by the form should have a basic relation to the monitoring objectives of the program. For example, the client characteristics recorded in the form should be directly related to program eligibility criteria, planning objectives, or decisions about intervention strategies. In other words, information should only be gathered if it can be used for monitoring or program operation.

b. Each form should contain sufficient identifying information so that information gathered during different contacts can be traced back to the same client. In most cases, a client's name and social security number are sufficient for these purposes.

c. Duplication of information should be avoided. Beyond the minimum essentials, identifying information, such as age, address, or occupation, need not be required on every agency form used or in every contact with the client.

d. For each category of information, a precise operational definition should be made to facilitate classification and tabulation of the data and to insure reliability.

e. Instructions should be included regarding appropriate sources of validation for information related to eligibility requirements, for example, birth certificate, driver's license, proof of residency or income status.

f. In counting frequency of client contacts, information should be gathered in such a way as to indicate whether client contacts were repeated contacts with the same clients or separate contacts with different clients. A program may serve 20 families with 5 interviews per family in a month or 100 families with 1 interview per family during the same time period. The total number of contacts is 100 in both cases, but the patterns of service are quite different. The service data should be collected so that these differences are discernible.

g. Operational definitions should be consistent on all forms and from one reporting period to another. This is particularly important in studying time trends and in cross-validating information received from clients. If the program data are to be compared with data from other programs, operational definitions should be consistent among the programs.

h. Provision should be made for validating the quality of the information obtained, that is, for monitoring the monitoring process. For example, a caseworker may record contacts with a client that the client denies took place. This discrepancy may result from different definitions of "contact" or from misrepresentation by one of the sources of information. Attempts should be made to spot-check the information-gathering process to determine the validity of the information gathered.

4. Collection of Client Census Data

To insure the collection of comparable and high-quality data, information should be gathered in a systematic fashion at standard points in the client's participation in the program. For example, information should be routinely collected at intake, at strategic times in the servicing of clients, and at termination and/or referral to other programs.

The persons recording the information should know the criteria for classifying and validating information as well as the purposes for which the information is needed. If more than one person collects information, attention should be given to the reliability of the different data collectors. Most importantly, if staff are to participate in data collection, they should understand its purpose, they should be committed to collecting complete and valid information, they should be trained to do it, they should have the time to do it, and they should be rewarded for doing it. The collection of information should not be so cumbersome that it interferes with service to clients. If any of the foregoing criteria are not met, the monitoring process will be undermined by staff.

**5. Comparison of Client Census Data with Program Objectives
   and Standards of Service**

Once data have been collected for a given time period, they should be
tabulated (specific techniques for data analysis will be discussed in chapter
9) and compared against planned program objectives and standards of service. No precise formula can be offered for determining whether a discrepancy between the census data and program objectives is too great. The chi-
square statistic (to be discussed in chapter 8) can be used to determine the
statistical significance of the difference between the program expectations
and the actual service data. However, this is an area in which a judgment
must be made about whether discrepancies are within tolerable limits and
about the causes of discrepancies between standards and agency performance. Perhaps modes of client recruitment are not right, or inappropriate
services are offered. Perhaps clients are having transportation difficulties or
problems getting to the agency during 9 to 5 office hours. The answers to
these questions may be determined by group discussions with staff, or
follow-up interviews with agency clientele or with people who were not
served by the agency but are part of the target population. If, however, standards of agency performance are being met, questions about expansion of
services and/or greater efficiency might be raised. None of the foregoing
questions should be approached without first conducting a client census.

HYPOTHETICAL ILLUSTRATION

PROBLEM SITUATION AND ADMINISTRATIVE TASK

A delinquency prevention agency receives funds for a job placement program in a small industrial city. Although service statistics have not been
compiled, the program's administrator has the impression that staff are most
responsive to and successful with middle-class, nonminority youngsters who
come to the agency to find summer jobs. From the standpoint of its overall
goal, delinquency prevention, it is felt that the program may not be serving
the right population. In addition, the funding source is asking for an accounting of how the agency is utilizing its resources, and some leaders of
the low-income community have begun to raise questions about the agency's
lack of responsiveness to low-income youngsters.

The administrator of the program decides to conduct a client census to determine the number and type of youngsters served. In addition, he would

like some data on the nature of program contact with different groups of youngsters.

PLANNING AND IMPLEMENTING A CLIENT CENSUS

1. Designation of the Target Population

The primary target population of the program is low-income, minority teenaged boys. This group is selected on the basis of the fact that they are vastly overrepresented in the juvenile crime statistics of the city.

2. Delineation of Program Objectives and Standards of Service

Juvenile court statistics indicate that 73 percent of the adjudicated delinquents in a city were from homes in which the annual income was less than $4,000 per year. Sixty-five percent were high school dropouts. Seventy percent were males. Forty-eight percent were black, 37 percent Chicano, and the remaining 15 percent were listed as white or "other." The program administrator decides that these percentages should be used as standards for determining whether or not the program is serving its intended clientele, that is, delinquency-prone youngsters. And, while the agency does not have quotas for various groups, it is felt that service statistics should at least resemble the profile of adjudicated delinquents.

3. Construction of Client Census Forms

It is decided that for properly monitoring the client population it would be important to collect data on the characteristics of clients who present themselves at intake, and of those who move on from intake to job counseling and placement sessions. Forms are developed for gathering information about family income, sex, race, and educational status. The initial information is routinely collected by intake workers. The names of youngsters who begin and those who complete the job counseling and placement sessions are matched with the information collected by intake workers.

4. Collection of Client Census Data

The information listed above is routinely collected by intake workers over a period of time that allows completion of a full cycle of intake, job counseling, and placement. The names of youngsters who began and those who completed the job counseling and placement sessions are then matched through code numbers with the information collected by intake workers.

Once this information is tabulated, it is possible to develop a profile of the social characteristics of youngsters who come to the program, of those who begin and of those who complete the sequence. In a study of program outcomes, one would also collect data on what happens to youngsters after they leave the program. However, resource limitations may make a follow-up study impossible.

The relevant sections of the intake monitoring form would look something like this:

Code number_____

1. Applicant's name: _____
                                        (write in)

2. Age on last birthday (check one):

    Under 14_____ 15_____ 16_____ 17_____ 18_____ 19_____ 20_____ 21 & over_____

3. Sex (check one):   Male_____   Female_____

4. Race (check one):   Black_____   Chicano_____   White_____   Other_____

5. Family income per year (check one):

    Under $4,000   _____
    $4,000 to 5,999   _____
    $6,000 to 7,999   _____
    Over $8,000   _____
    Don't know   _____

6. Last year of education completed (check one):

    Less than eighth grade   _____
    Eighth grade   _____
    Ninth grade   _____
    Tenth grade   _____
    Eleventh grade   _____
    High school grad   _____
    Some college   _____

7. Current school status (check one):

    Enrolled in school and attending   _____
    Enrolled in school and not attending   _____
    Suspended   _____
    Expelled from school   _____
    Dropped out voluntarily   _____

Other sections of the questionnaire would include questions about educational and occupational aspirations, previous work experience, work-relevant skills, and other information that would be useful in job counseling and placement. It would also record the intake worker's disposition of the case and the reasons for screening out any who were not allowed to continue in the program.

5. Comparison of Client Census Data with Program Objectives and Standards of Service

After the data are collected, it is possible to compare actual patterns of service with program expectancies. By tabulating the percentages in each data category at the three critical points in the careers of program participants, one can show the percentages of program participants in each income category who completed each phase of agency service.

Table 6.1 shows the percentage of program participants who completed each phase of client processing by family income. It also compares the income data for program participants with income data for adjudged delinquents, the standard against which agency performance is measured. The findings show that the program is attracting relatively high proportions of low-income youngsters. Of those seen at intake 61 percent have family incomes of less than $4,000 per year. This comes fairly close to meeting the 73 percent criterion established by the delinquency statistics. It indicates that recruitment strategies, advertising, referral, and outreach efforts are working fairly well.

Table 6.1
Percentage of Program Participants
and Adjudicated Delinquents by Family Income

Family Income	Seen at Intake	Began Counseling	Completed Counseling	Adjudicated Delinquents
Under $4,000	61%	58%	29%	73%
$4–5,999	21%	25%	18%	11%
$6–7,999	8%	6%	20%	10%
Over $8,000	8%	10%	31%	5%
Don't know	2%	1%	2%	1%
Total %	100%	100%	100%	100%
Number	581	460	237	3,481

Table 6.1 also shows us that a relatively high proportion (58 percent) of those who begin job counseling and placement sessions are from the lowest income category. In addition, comparing the total number who were seen at intake (581) with the number of those who began job counseling and training sessions (460), we note that only 121 youngsters dropped out or were screened out of the program at intake. These findings suggest that intake workers were successful in encouraging low-income youngsters to remain in the program and were generally able to sustain the interest of most of the youngsters seen at intake.

However, we see a dramatic decline in the proportion of youngsters from low-income homes who completed counseling and placement sessions (from 58 to 29 percent). A comparison of those in the higher income brackets indicates a correlative increase for those from families with incomes over $6,000 per year (from 16 to 51 percent). Overall, looking at the total number who started and completed the sessions, we see that 223 youngsters dropped out of the sessions, almost half of those who started them.

This suggests to the administrator that there is something about these sessions that is turning low-income youngsters off the program.

By making similar comparisons using client census data based on race, sex, educational level, and so on, he is able to corroborate his suspicion that the job counseling and placement sessions are causing youngsters from the target population to drop out of the program.

The causes of this pattern may have to do with staff attitudes, staff skills, the type of programming offered, the kinds of jobs that are provided. In order to determine what is causing this negative pattern, the program administrator may begin systematic observations of the job counseling and placement sessions, interview staff, send questionnaires to program dropouts, and so on. Once questions are answered, decisions can be made about how to correct the pattern.

Whatever the causes, the monitoring of quantitative client information has provided a useful picture of program performance. Moreover, it has located areas of success and failure in service to the program's target population. Finally, the client census has increased administrative control in the interest of achieving program goals.

EXERCISE

Select an agency or program that has service delivery objectives. On the basis of your knowledge of agency objectives, official documents, interviews with staff and administrators, articulate two measurable standards of service delivery to the program's target population. Determine whether the program routinely collects data on service delivery. If it does not, develop a form for doing so. Collect the data for a specified period of time. Tabulate your findings and compare them with the service standards you established earlier. How do the findings compare with the standards you articulated? What implications can you draw from the findings? What sorts of corrections or changes, if any, seem to be suggested?

SELECTED BIBLIOGRAPHY

Goldstein, Harris K. *Research Standards and Methods for Social Workers.* New Orleans, La.: The Hauser Press, 1963; pp. 45–54, 71–82.

Isaac, Stephen, with William B. Michael. *Handbook in Research and Evaluation.* San Diego, Cal.: Robert R. Knapp, 1971; pp. 162–71.

Terry, George R. *Principles of Management.* 6th ed. Homewood, Ill.: Richard D. Irwin, 1972; pp. 220–49, 535–57.

Weiss, Carol H. *Evaluation Research.* Englewood Cliffs, N.J.: Prentice-Hall, 1972; pp. 24–59.

Weiss, Robert S. *Statistics in Social Research.* New York: John Wiley and Sons, 1968; pp. 178–87.

CHAPTER SEVEN

Using Forms to Monitor Staff Activities

IN THE PRECEDING CHAPTER, we showed how forms and monitoring procedures could be used to study program contact with clients. This chapter is concerned with ways in which forms and monitoring procedures can be used to gather data about how staff use their time. *Time and activity* studies rely on research concepts and principles discussed in previous chapters, and also draw on ideas from administrative science and human engineering.

Time and activity studies describe the number and types of activities in which selected staff are engaged within specified units of time. This information is then related to performance standards and program objectives. In such studies, the monitoring process is used for *quantity control* of staff performance. Here the monitoring process involves the designation of the population of staff or staff units to be studied; the selection of a time frame within which staff activities will be recorded; the delineation of standards of staff performance in relation to program objectives; the selection of time and activity measures; the construction of appropriate forms with which to record the information; collection and analysis of the information; and comparison of this data with predetermined standards of staff performance. As a result of this monitoring, adjustments can be made in staff assignments, allocation of staff resources, and so on.

MONITORING STAFF ACTIVITIES AND SOCIAL PROGRAM ADMINISTRATION

In chapter 6, we noted the increasing pressures placed on social agencies for accountability. In that chapter, we emphasized the demand for documentation of service delivery to particular client groups. Another way in which the pressure for accountability expresses itself is in the demand for documentation of staff activities and of the relative efficiency of the ways in which staff activities are organized. Administrators are frequently required to demonstrate to funding sources how program personnel are spending their work time. For cost accounting purposes, time and activity data are used to estimate the costs in time and money of different aspects of staff performance.

Beyond the issue of accountability, effective administration requires reliable and valid information about the collective efforts of staff. This information is helpful in making decisions about the structuring and restructuring of staff activities. It helps determine whether staff activities are directly related to program goals. It can reveal unnecessary duplication of effort. It can be used to determine whether unskilled staff are performing functions beyond their skills, or conversely, whether skilled staff are using their time in activities that can be successfully accomplished by workers with less training and experience. Time and activity studies can be used to monitor individual performance and to make decisions about individual worker assignments, rewards, and sanctions. Finally, while time and activity studies do not evaluate the effectiveness of program intervention, they do provide essential descriptive information about program effort.

PRINCIPLES FOR CONDUCTING TIME AND ACTIVITY STUDIES

1. Designation of the Staff Population to Be Studied

In time and activity studies, the objects of study are staff. Some studies include the entire staff. In others, particular staff units or levels in the organizational hierarchy are singled out for scrutiny. For example, in a comprehensive study of staff activity, one might look at the efforts of administration, supervisors, line workers, volunteers, clerical staff. In less comprehensive studies, the activities of only those paid workers who have direct contact with clients may be considered.

The choice of the population to be studied depends on the intended scope of the monitoring effort, the size and scope of the program itself, the number and range of functions performed by staff, the amount and type of information desired, and the resources available for staff monitoring.

2. Selection of a Time Frame for the Study

The *time frame* for the study refers to the duration of time within which data will be collected. A time and activity study may be based on a day's, a month's, or a year's activities. The decision is based on the availability of resources for monitoring as well as on the time it takes for staff to complete the full range of its functions.

In general, the time frame selected for a time and activity study should correspond to that used for recording client contacts. Thus, if statistics on client processing are recorded for a given month, a time and activity study should represent the same month. In this way, the two different sets of data can be related to each other. Overall, the time frames for reporting all agency statistics should be comparable.

3. Delineation of Standards of Staff Performance

Job descriptions generally describe the range of activities or functions required of a given organizational position. Typically, however, job descriptions do not specify the amounts of time that staff members are expected to devote to these different activities. Nor do they typically rank the functions in terms of organizational priorities.

In newly developing programs, where there are no traditional performance norms, the amount of time devoted to different tasks may depend on particular developmental needs of the program. Here, for example, staff may spend more time recruiting clients than serving them.

In programs in which staff performance is not highly visible, the amount of time devoted to different tasks may depend on the worker's perception of which tasks are most personally rewarding, for example, seeing clients rather than processing forms.

Worker efforts to allocate their time may also be based on sound knowledge and experience about the best way to structure their various activities.

Nevertheless, the administrator (possibly in consultation with relevant staff) should make an effort to delineate expected standards of worker performance. This is done by first identifying the range of functions and activities associated with each position. These functions are then rank ordered, from highest to lowest, in terms of the amount of time that should be allocated to each.

Social workers in residential treatment centers for children, for example, may be expected to do the following: provide direct counseling to children in placement, provide counseling for families of children in placement, provide counseling to cottage parents, be in contact with outside agencies that will facilitate a child's return to the community, make home visits to assess the readiness of the home for the child's return, maintain contact with other relevant staff within the agency about a child's progresss, receive supervision, prepare monthly statistical reports, maintain process records on client progress, and so on. On the basis of their relation to program objectives, these functions could then be ranked from those to which social workers are expected to devote most time to those that rank lowest in time priority.

4. Selection of Time Units

The variable of time is easily operationalized in terms of seconds, minutes, and hours. However, in conducting time and activity studies a unit of time must be selected within which activities will be recorded. This is not so easy. For most social agency tasks, a second is obviously too short and a day too long. For many programs, there are time-structured activities that can serve as a guide for selecting the proper time unit. More typically, workers are asked to record their activities at 15-minute intervals throughout the day. Or, they may be given a list of job-related activities and asked to indicate how many minutes per day or hours per week are spent engaged in each of the activities. Another common unit of measurement is the percentage of time out of a total work week spent on designated functions.

5. Selection of Activity Measures

Activity measures, like any other empirical measures, should be classified into mutually exclusive and exhaustive categories. The categories should refer to the major functions and activities included in the job description for a given position. Categories should not be so broad as to miss important distinctions between different aspects of the job. For example, the term "counseling" could refer to work with clients, their families, or their peers. Such an activity category would be too broad to indicate important differences in caseworker activity.

Alternatively, categories should not be so specific as to prevent aggregation of the information. For example, a marriage counselor may, in the course of a given time period, treat many different kinds of sexual dysfunction. For monitoring purposes, it would probably not be necessary to record data on the specific forms of dysfunction that were treated.

6. Construction of Time and Activity Forms

The principles that apply to the construction of questionnaires, interview schedules, and client census forms apply to time and activity forms as well.

Measures should be operationally specific, valid, and reliable. But in contrast with the techniques previously discusssed, time and activity forms are specifically directed to obtaining information about staff performance. In monitoring efforts designed to generate information about overall program effectiveness, data concerning output measures may also be collected. In such studies, workers may be asked to record not only their activities but the numbers of cases opened, closed, referred, and so on. Whatever their specific purpose, staff time and activity forms should be constructed with the following principles in mind:

a. The forms should be simple, clear, and easy to use. They should employ a language that is familiar to and used by workers in describing their work activities.

b. Each form should contain sufficient identifying information so that data gathered during different time intervals can be traced back to the same worker.

c. For each category of information required, there should be an operational definition to facilitate valid and reliable staff reporting.

d. Operational definitions should be consistent on all forms, from one time interval to another and from one staff position to another. This makes it possible to monitor individual changes in performance over time as well as to locate possible duplication of effort by workers in different positions.

e. The time unit to be used should be clearly specified and consistent on all forms. Moreover, the form should cover *all* work time, both to create a complete record of worker performance and to assure adequate and common bases for percentage comparisons.

f. Provisions should be made for validating the information obtained from workers. This may be done by checking the internal consistency of responses. Additional validation may come from comparing worker self-reports with other, more objective data of cases closed, clients referred, and so on. Here other forms may be used to validate self-reported behavior.

7. The Collection of Time and Activity Data

To insure the collection of comparable and high-quality data, procedures should be worked out so that workers can record their activities as soon after completion as possible. This may require keeping a form on the desk at all times so that activity categories such as phone calls can be checked immediately and not forgotten.

For weekly or monthly data, workers may be asked to keep daily diaries of their activities, which they cumulate at the end of a given time period. This procedure is time-consuming but yields more reliable results than relying on subjective impression and memory.

The staff participating in the study should know the purposes for which the information is required. They should be committed to complete and accurate recording of their activities. They should be briefed on how to do it, given the time to do it, and rewarded for completion of their task. As with client census procedures, the collection of staff time and activity data should not seriously interfere with service delivery. Otherwise, the monitoring process will be subverted by staff.

8. Comparison of Time and Activity Data with Program Objectives and Performance Standards

Once the data have been collected, they should be tabulated (see chapter 9) and compared against program objectives and performance standards. Here again, no precise formula can be offered for determining whether a discrepancy between staff performance and program expectancies is too great. Reasonable judgments must be made.

In addition to helping to assess the efforts of staff units, these data provide important information about individual performance. For example, by comparing individual performance data with the total performance data for workers in a category, it is possible to identify these workers whose performance in critical areas is far below or far above average. By looking at performance data for the same workers over time, one can establish whether individual workers are improving or falling down in critical areas of job functioning.

Moreoover, by comparing the activities of workers in different job categories, with different performance expectations, one is able to identify areas of overlap or duplication of services.

These and many other administrative uses can be made of information gathered by systematic monitoring of staff activity.

HYPOTHETICAL ILLUSTRATION

PROBLEM SITUATION AND ADMINISTRATIVE TASK

A community public health program is set up in a rural area to provide clients with family planning counseling, contraceptive materials, and prenatal care. The area is economically depressed and characterized by a high birth rate and a high rate of infant mortality.

Besides an administrator, a consulting physician, and a small clerical staff, the core staff of the program includes eight paraprofessional health workers and four public health nurses. The paraprofessionals, recruited from the local community, are expected to do outreach work. More specifically, their task involves house-to-house canvassing, informing families about available services, and encouraging them to make use of these services. The public health nurses are responsible for family planning counseling and education, distribution of contraceptive materials, routine prenatal examinations, and supervision of the paraprofessionals.

The program itself is housed in the Health Department building in the local county seat. The target population of approximately 5,000 families lives on small farms, scattered throughout this rural mountainous area.

After two years' operation, county health officials note that rates of birth and infant mortality have not declined, despite the fact that agency statistics showed the program to have "served" over 2,000 families. The administrator decides to initiate a time and activity study to monitor the efforts of staff.

PLANNING AND IMPLEMENTING A TIME
AND ACTIVITY STUDY

1. Designation of the Staff Population to be Studied

The administrator decides that paraprofessionals and public health nurses are the core of the program and that their on-the-job activities should be systematically monitored.

2. Selection of a Time Frame for the Study

Since the program must report monthly service statistics to its funding source, it is decided that the time frame for the study should be one month. This makes possible a matching of service statistics with time and activity data and offers a measure of the reliability of both sets of data.

3. Delineation of Standards of Staff Performance

Using program goals as a guide, the administrator determines that the major responsibilities of paraprofessional staff can be ranked from highest to lowest as follows:

1. recruitment of clientele
2. client follow-up visits
3. referral of clientele to other programs

4. travel
5. receiving supervision
6. administrative and clerical work.

The major responsibilities of the public health nursing staff are ranked as follows:

1. family planning counseling
2. prenatal counseling
3. physical examinations
4. referral activities with clients
5. supervision of paraprofessionals
6. administrative and clerical work
7. contact with other agencies.

These rank orderings are a rough guide to the functional priorities for each position. They do not indicate exactly how much time should be spent on any of these activities.

4. Selection of Time Units

After a number of possibilities are considered, it is decided that workers' time and activity should be expressed as percentages of time out of their total week spent on each of these functions.

5. Selection of Activity Measures

Operational definitions of the functions listed above are developed and discussed with staff to eliminate ambiguities.

6. Construction of Time and Activity Forms

Using the functional categories identified earlier, a common form is developed for use by both professionals and paraprofessionals. The form looks something like this:

Staff Time and Activity Form

Please indicate the percentage of time you spent in the past week on each of these activities. Thank you.

Client Contact	*Percent*
1. Recruitment of new clients	_____
2. Family planning counseling	_____

3. Prenatal counseling   _____
4. Physical examinations   _____
5. Client follow-up   _____
6. Referral activities with clients   _____

           Total client contact   _____

          Supervision   *Percent*

1. Receive supervision   _____
2. Provide supervision   _____

           Total supervision   _____

      Administrative and Clerical   *Percent*

1. Record keeping   _____
2. Staff meetings   _____
3. Contact with other agencies   _____

     Total administrative and clerical   _____

      Travel and Other Activities   *Percent*

1. Travel   _____

2. Other (write in)   _____

3. Other (write in)   _____

     Total travel and other activities   _____
     Total weekly activities   100%

The "other" write-in spaces are provided for job activities that are significant but that the administrator did not anticipate in constructing the time and activity form. In situations where the administrator does not have adequate knowledge of a job to construct a list of activities and priorities, an initial study phase may be necessary in which workers are asked to keep diaries of their activities, which become the basis for the development of activity categories. Alternatively, observation approaches may be used to identify significant activity categories.

7. Collection of Time and Activity Data

To facilitate reliable reporting, workers are encouraged to keep a daily diary that indicates their activities at 15-minute time intervals. Diary notebooks and paper with appropriate time intervals are provided for this

purpose. At the end of each week, for four weeks, workers are asked to tabulate their weekly activities in percentages and record them on the time and
activity form provided.

8. Comparison of Time and Activity Data with Program Objectives and Performance Standards

When the data have been collected, it is possible to compare staff activity
with program expectancies. More specifically, the following questions can
be considered: (1) Do the activities and time allocations for paraprofessionals and public health nurses correspond with administrative expectancies? (2) Do the activities of paraprofessionals and public health nurses
overlap more than they should? (3) Do the activities of the two groups vary
or remain constant throughout the month? (4) Are the activities and time
allocations of individuals within each group far below or far above administrative expectations and actual performance patterns of the group itself?

The findings of the four-week study, aggregated for each group, are presented in table 7.1. Note that the patterns for individual workers have been
left out of this table. If space and time permitted, these could be included for
assessment of individual performance.

The findings in table 7.1 reveal a pattern of staff activity and time use that
departs considerably from administrative expectancies. Overall we see public health nurses heavily involved in client follow-up and referral activities
and in administrative, supervisory, and clerical tasks. A relatively small percentage of their time is spent in performing their primary functions of family
planning counseling, prenatal counseling, and physical exams.

Performance of paraprofessionals appears closer to what was expected of
them, although a few appear to be doing counseling. This is clearly outside
of their job definition. Relatively little of their time is spent in follow-up activities, which probably explains the high numbers of client contact for the
total agency but the small proportion of clients contacted who ultimately
come to the agency for service. Moreover, the data on follow-up activities
of public health nurses suggest that many clients who do come for a first
agency contact do not return. In addition, the relatively high level of referral
activity suggests that of those who come, many have problems that require
services of other agencies. This may be because they are multiproblem cases
or because they were not properly recruited in the first place.

Public health nurses are also seen spending an inordinate amount of time

Table 7.1

Monthly Percentage of Work Time Spent in Each Activity by Paraprofessionals and
Public Health Nurses

Client Related Activities	*Para-professionals*	*Public Health Nurses*
1. Recruitment of clients	40	3
2. Family planning counseling	2	8
3. Prenatal counseling	2	9
4. Physical examinations	—	5
5. Client follow-up	5	15
6. Referral activities with clients	10	15
Total	59%	55%
Supervision		
1. Receive supervision	10	—
2. Provide supervision	—	16
Total	10%	16%
Administrative and Clerical		
1. Record keeping	5	5
2. Staff meetings	2	15
3. Contact with other agencies	3	9
Total	10%	29%
Travel and Other Activities		
1. Travel	20	—
2. Other	1	—
3. Other	—	—
Total	21%	—

in staff meetings. This may be a euphemism for spending time with other
staff while waiting for something to do.

These time and activity patterns strongly suggest the need for structural
reorganization of the program. After checking out a number of the possible
implications of the findings with staff, a decision is made to have public
health nurses and paraprofessionals work as outreach teams. The teams
would travel in pairs, making home visits, follow-up visits, and so on
without requiring clients to make the trip into the city for service. Although
this creates some dissatisfaction among some of the professional nurses, it is

likely to increase overall program efficiency and the quality of service provided.

EXERCISE

Select a social program or staff unit within a program. Using the job descriptions of staff in at least two positions, list in order of administrative priority the activities that make up their jobs. Devise a time and activity form and procedures for implementing it for a one-week period. Analyze the findings and decide what, if any, changes are suggested by the findings.

SELECTED BIBLIOGRAPHY

Billingsley, Andrew. "The Role of the Social Worker in a Child Protective Agency," in Tony Tripodi, Phillip Fellin, and Henry J. Meyer, *The Assessment of Social Research*. Itasca, Ill.: F. E. Peacock, 1969; pp. 183–95.

Drucker, Peter F. *Management: Tasks, Responsibilities, Practices*. New York: Harper and Row, 1973; pp. 494–505.

Elkin, Robert F. *Analyzing Time, Costs and Operations in a Voluntary Children's Institution and Agency*. Washington, D.C.: U.S. Department of Health, Education, and Welfare, 1965; 68 pp.

Hill, John G. "Cost Analysis of Social Work Service," in Norman A. Polansky, ed., *Social Work Research*. Chicago: University of Chicago Press, 1960; pp. 238–44.

Terry, George R. *Principles of Management*. 6th ed. Homewood, Ill.: Richard D. Irwin, 1972; pp. 603–18.

CHAPTER EIGHT

Using Sampling in Monitoring Staff Performance

SAMPLING IS A TECHNIQUE for increasing the efficiency of data gathering. When properly employed, it enables a researcher to make relatively safe generalizations about a larger *target population* from findings within a smaller *sample* taken from the target population. The greater the similarity between the sample and the target population, the safer the generalizations that can be made. When sample and target populations are demonstrated to be highly comparable, we refer to the sample as being *representative*.

Many of the concepts and techniques used in sampling are designed either to increase the chances of drawing a representative sample or to decrease the cost of data gathering. Unfortunately, however, these two objectives are generally in conflict. The larger the sample, the greater the likelihood of representativeness, but the greater the cost of data collection as well. This contradiction is a continuing dilemma for the researcher who does not have the resources to study an entire target population. Here a sampling strategy must be devised that both maximizes the chances of representativeness and remains within the resource limitations of the study. Even after the sample has been drawn, however, statistical techniques must be used to determine whether the strategy has in fact produced a representative sample.

This chapter describes a range of sampling techniques that can be used in connection with program monitoring. The sampling strategies discussed vary in cost and in likelihood of generating a representative sample. A simple statistical test, the chi-square, is introduced as a test for representativeness.

SAMPLING TECHNIQUES AND SOCIAL
PROGRAM ADMINISTRATION

Sampling techniques are useful for gathering data relevant to all aspects of social program administration. In planning, for example, an administrator may not have sufficient resources to survey an entire potential client population concerning their service needs. Instead, a carefully drawn sample of a certain proportion of potential clients may be interviewed. Once it is determined that this sample is representative of the larger target population, then relatively safe generalizations can be made about service needs of the latter.

In monitoring, sampling may be used in connection with interviews, questionnaires, or time and activity data to monitor staff performance, Thus, an administrator may want to know whether outreach workers are making sufficient contacts with the client community. Rather than surveying the entire client population to determine whether contacts have been made, he may have a sample of the client population interviewed or sent questionnaires asking for this information. If staff time and activity data are available but too copious for complete analysis, a representative sample of this data can be analyzed to reveal the proportion of staff time spent in client contact activities.

In program evaluation, follow-up studies may be conducted with data gathered from a representative sample of former agency clients. Since resources for program evaluation are seldom sufficient for a study of all former clients, sampling is frequently necessary.

In the preceding chapter, we showed how time and activity data can be used to monitor the sheer quantity of staff activity or input into a program. We referred to that as quantity control. In this chapter, we apply sampling concepts and techniques to monitoring the *quality* of program input, and this can be regarded as *quality control*.

SAMPLING PRINCIPLES

1. Designation of the Target Population and Sampling Unit

As we stated in chapter 6, the target population is that population to which a program is directing its efforts. Ideally, it has been specified during program planning. Social agencies may direct their efforts toward different kinds of target populations, for example, community organizations, groups, families, individuals.

In order to draw a sample population, one must first determine the basic units from which to choose. The type of target population determines the *sampling unit*. Thus, if the target of program intervention is families, then families are the sampling units. If the target population is every adult residing in a given locality, then each person in this category represents a sampling unit. To increase the chances that the sample population will be unbiased and representative, each sampling unit should have an equal probability of being included in the sample. Not all sampling strategies make this possible, however.

2. Choosing a Sampling Strategy

There are basically two kinds of sampling strategies—*nonprobability* and *probability* sampling. In nonprobability sampling, there is no way of determining the probability that any particular sampling unit will actually be included in the sample population. Nonprobability sampling techniques are cheap and quick, but more likely to produce biased and nonrepresentative samples.

Some types of nonprobability sampling strategies are accidental sampling, quota sampling, and purposive sampling. *Accidental sampling* involves choosing the most readily accessible set of sampling units available, without regard to whether the sampling units drawn are representative of the target population. For example, in a client evaluation of services received, an administrator may not have enough money to pay interviewers to contact every client seen during the past year. Instead, he may have interviews conducted with the next 100 clients served by the agency. The study could be done within the confines of the agency, over a short period of time, in a context that would facilitate respondent compliance. However, the findings of such a study would probably be highly unreliable. Safe inferences could not be drawn from it to the target population of clients served by the agency, primarily because the sample population was selected in a manner that would be likely to introduce bias into the findings. The clients drawn in this accidental sample may be very different than those who came before them because of seasonal differences in the kinds of problems clients present at different times of the year. The quality of services they receive may be different, since those who come later benefit from the experience gathered by program staff over the course of a year. The responses these clients give may be different because they are currently receiving service rather than having completed their agency contacts. For these and other reasons, the findings of a study based on such a sample could not be generalized to the target population served by the agency over the past year.

A second type of nonprobability sampling is *quota sampling*. It is a more refined form of accidental sampling and is frequently used in less scientific public opinion polls. In quota sampling, the target population is classified by certain pertinent properties such as race, ethnicity, age. Quotas are then set, frequently based upon the proportion of each group in the target population. Thus if blacks constitute 10 percent of the target population served by an agency, a quota sample of 100 clients should contain 10 blacks. Once this quota is achieved, interviewers are instructed to not include any more blacks in the sample population. This strategy produces a sample population that resembles the target population in the properties specified. However, since the selection of respondents is based on easy accessibility, the result is still likely to be biased and unrepresentative. All blacks in the target population do not have an equal chance at being selected. Moreover, in quota sampling those who refuse to respond are simply ignored. This is why public opinion polls are frequently wrong.

Purposive sampling is a third type of nonprobability sampling. It involves hand selecting cases for inclusion in the sample population on the basis of some notion of what is typical. Like accidental and quota sampling, it is cheap and quick. It is also highly unreliable, since it is frequently based on erroneous stereotypes. As a result, the researcher's biases are introduced into the sample and the findings of such a study will reinforce erroneous assumptions.

Probability sampling strategies make it possible to calculate the probability that any one sampling unit in the total target population will be selected for the sample. Moreover, probability sampling makes it possible to calculate the margin of error that is likely to occur under different sampling conditions and the sample size that is necessary to reduce error to a tolerable minimum. In other words, probability sampling enables the researcher to estimate the degree to which generalizations to the target population can be made safely from findings within the sample population. Though they cannot guarantee the selection of a representative sample population, probability sampling strategies greatly increase the likelihood of this outcome.

The most common type of probability sampling strategy is the *simple random sample*. With this strategy, every unit within the target population has an equal probability of being included in the sample population. Each unit within the target population is assigned a number. Then, using a table of random numbers, the researcher selects individual units randomly for the sample population. This technique requires no previous knowledge about the target population, but is more likely to produce a representative sample than any of the nonprobability sampling strategies. Even simple random sampling, however, does not insure representativeness.

Another form of probability sampling is *systematic sampling*. This technique is particularly useful in sampling case records that are filed either alphabetically or numerically. To do systematic sampling, one must first establish the sampling ratio, that is, the proportion of the total target population that will be included in the sample population. For example, an agency researcher may decide on a sampling ratio of 1/4. Then, taking a random starting point, he selects every fourth case record until he completes one full cycle of all case records. If there were 1,000 case records, he has selected a systematic sample of 25 cases for the sample population. Here again, representativeness is not assured but it is much more likely than if he had simply selected the first 250 case records in the file.

A more refined kind of probability sampling is *stratified random sampling*. In this sampling strategy, the target population is first described according to certain pertinent properties—for example, race, ethnicity, organizational rank. If race is considered to be the most pertinent property, the target population is first separated by racial grouping. Then a random sample is selected from within each racial grouping. The numbers chosen from each group may correspond to the proportion of the group in the total target population. Here, we speak of *proportionate stratified random sampling*. In some cases, the researcher may want to overrepresent particular groups for closer study. For example, in a study of staff, a researcher may randomly select 1/10 of the direct service workers, 1/5 of the supervisors, and 1/2 of the administrative personnel. Here, we speak of *disproportionate* stratified random sampling. Because the numbers of personnel in each group are different to begin with, a disproportionate sampling strategy may be used to generate a sample population with equal numbers of direct service workers, supervisors, and administrative personnel. Such a strategy implies that members of different organizational strata have different probabilities of being included in the sample population, but the probabilities for individuals within each stratum are known. This is not the case in quota sampling.

Depending on the nature of the study, any of the foregoing sampling strategies may be used on a one-time, multiple, or sequential basis. Overall, it is clear that the advantages of probability sampling far outweigh the disadvantages. Consequently, the remainder of our discussion will focus on systematic, simple random, and stratified random sampling techniques. When in doubt, however, a simple random sample should be the strategy of choice.

3. Selecting a Sample Size

The decision about the size of the sample population is a complex one. Some aspects of this decision are highly technical and may require the consultation of a researcher. This is particularly true when one wants a precise estimate of the possibility of making an erroneous generalization from a sample population of a given size to a target population of a given size.*

Other aspects of this decision are more practical. These involve questions of resources. How much time and money are available and how many interviews do they make possible in a day? What is the response rate likely to be? What will be the cost per completed interview? More often than not, these practical considerations will determine the sample size.

Recognizing the inevitability of the above, we suggest two rough rules of thumb. First, do not choose samples smaller than 50. Second, if there are categories of sampling units that are particularly relevant to the study, include at least 25 units of each of these categories in the sample population. So in a study of interventions of social workers in 1,000 cases, choose at least 1/20 of the cases for direct scrutiny. If the study focuses on the quality of intervention with middle-class versus lower-class clientele, be sure that the sampling strategy provides at least 25 cases of each.

4. Listing the Target Population

Once a sampling strategy has been chosen, a complete list of the target population should be compiled. For systematic sampling, sampling units should be listed in alphabetic order or any other order that does not involve an implicit socially relevant pattern. If a simple random sample is to be selected, all that is required is a complete list of the target population. The ordering of units is of no significance, since each individual unit chosen for the sample population will be chosen randomly. For stratified random sam-

---

* For the formula for calculating the size of the sample required on the basis of size of target population and tolerable margin of error, see Walker and Lev, *Statistical Inference,* p. 70.

pling, a separate but complete list should be compiled for each stratum in the target population. Thus, if the sample population is going to be stratified by sex, then separate lists should be compiled for males and females. The ordering within these lists will be of no significance, since random selection will take place from within each stratum.

5. Selecting the Sample Population

As stated earlier, for systematic sampling a sampling ratio must be established. If the sampling ratio were 1/3, one would take a random starting point on the list of the target population and then select every third unit until the complete list has been gone through. If the sampling ratio were 1/8, one would take a random starting point and choose every eighth case.

In simple random sampling, the selection of sample units requires the use of a table of random numbers. These tables are lists of randomly generated numbers and are available in the appendices of most statistical textbooks. The following might be a column in one such table:

$$1009$$
$$3754$$
$$0852$$
$$9901$$
$$1280$$
$$\cdot \ \cdot \ \cdot \ \cdot$$
$$\cdot \ \cdot \ \cdot \ \cdot$$
$$\cdot \ \cdot \ \cdot \ \cdot$$

Each unit in the target population should then be numbered. If there are 5,000 cases, they should be numbered from 0,001 to 5,000. Taking a random starting point in the table of random numbers, one would then determine which cases will be drawn. The process continues until the required sample size is achieved. As an illustration, imagine a target population of 5,000 and a required sample size of 1,000. If the random starting point on the table of random numbers began with those listed above, we would include in our sample population cases numbered 1009, 3754, 0852, 9901, and so on. Numbers exceeding 5,000 would be ignored. Numbers that repeated themselves would be used only once. The process would continue until 1,000 cases were selected.

For stratified random sampling, a comparable set of procedures would be employed for each stratum of the target population until the desired sub-samples were selected.

6. Checking the Representativeness of the Sample

Since probability sampling does not insure representativeness, it is important that a sample population be checked to see whether it is representative of the target population on dimensions that are relevant to the study. This process requires some knowledge of the characteristics of both the sample and the target population.

To check for representativeness one begins with percentage comparisons between the sample and target populations on those dimensions that are relevant to the study and about which there is complete information for both populations. For example, a target population of 1,000 agency clients may contain 40 percent males and 60 percent females. A perfect, representative sample of 100 clients would contain 40 males and 60 females. If the sample population contained 25 males and 75 females, one would question the representativeness of the sample. In this case, males would be underrepresented and females overrepresented.

A second, more refined technique for assessing representativeness of a sample involves use of the chi-square (χ^2) statistic. This is a simple yet highly versatile statistic that has, among its many uses, the capacity to determine whether data distributions in the sample population are sufficiently like those in the target population to warrant the assumption of representativeness. Obversely, the chi-square statistic tells the researcher whether the sample population is significantly different from the target population, so that the assumption of representativeness must be rejected. Chi-square is based on a formula that contrasts the actual, observed frequencies in the sample population with those one would expect to find in a perfect representative sample. If the computed value of the chi-square is sufficiently low, a high degree of similarity between sample and target populations is indicated. This means that the sample population is representative on the dimensions tested and that relatively safe generalizations can be made from the findings within the sample population to the larger target population.

Let us take an example. Suppose we were comparing the sex distribution of the target population of agency clients referred to above with a 10 percent simple random sample population of 45 males and 55 females. Given the distribution in the target population, the expected frequencies for a perfect representative sample would be 40 males and 60 females. In tabular form, the actual and expected frequencies would look like this:

	Males	Females
Observed sample population	45	55
Expected sample population	40	60

Letters are assigned to the cells in the table:

	Males	Females
Observed sample population	O_m	O_f
Expected sample population	E_m	E_f

The formula for computing the chi-square for a table of these proportions * is:

$$\chi^2 = \frac{(O_m - E_m)^2}{E_m} + \frac{(O_f - E_f)^2}{E_f}$$

Substituting the numerical values from our expected and observed sample populations for the letters in the formula, we get:

$$\chi^2 = \frac{(45-40)^2}{40} + \frac{(55-60)^2}{60}$$

$$\chi^2 = \frac{25}{40} + \frac{25}{60}$$

$$\chi^2 = 1.04$$

With a table of these proportions, a chi-square with any value less than 3.84 is generally taken to indicate that the sample population is not significantly different from the target population.† Since the value of the chi-square in

---

* For tables with more than 2 pairs of expected and observed frequencies, the formula is simply extended to include the sum total of the squares of the differences between all pairs of observed and expected frequencies, divided by the expected frequencies for each pair. For tables with expected values below 5 in any cell, additional adjustments have to be made in the formula. Any basic statistics textbook will provide the appropriate formulas for these different conditions.

† With a table of these proportions, chi-square values that are 3.84 or greater are likely to occur by chance only 5 times in 100. According to research conventions, this probability level is considered to be statistically significant. Discussions of levels of statistical significance are contained in standard texts on statistical methods.

our example is only 1.04, we can assume that at least insofar as sex is concerned, our sample population *is* representative.

Hypothetical Illustration

PROBLEM SITUATION AND ADMINISTRATIVE TASK

An administrator in a state Department of Public Health is charged with the responsibility of licensing and monitoring the quality of services provided in state-run and proprietory nursing homes. In the state, there are 3,600 nursing homes. Of these, 1,200 are state operated and 2,400 are privately owned and operated.

In the past, each of these facilities has been routinely visited once a year for monitoring of health and hygiene standards, staff-patient ratios, staff qualifications, and so on. However, because of limitations in resources, these efforts were relatively superficial. Moreover, the administrator suspects that many of the facilities get spruced up for their annual visits and lapse into substandard care between visits. Following from this concern, the administrator decides to initiate a system of spot-checking nursing homes at unexpected times throughout the year and examining each in greater depth. Resources do not allow for examining all nursing homes. As a result, a sampling strategy is necessary for choosing which nursing homes will be monitored twice.

DEVELOPING A SAMPLING PLAN

1. Designation of the Target Population and Sampling Unit

In this example, the target population is the 3,600 nursing homes that are currently licensed and operating in the state. Each nursing home, whether state or privately run, constitutes a sampling unit.

2. Choosing a Sampling Strategy

The administrator realizes that if he is to get the greatest possible benefit from spot-checking, a representative sample of nursing homes should be visited. Therefore, he rejects a suggestion that staff ''randomly'' select nursing homes for spot-checking. He does this because he knows that staff will choose on an accidental rather than a truly random basis and because he is concerned that they may be biased in their selection of facilities for double monitoring. Staff may choose those facilities that are closest to the home office, or those that are most pleasant to visit. Alternatively, they may be biased in the opposite direction, choosing those facilities that appeared to have the most problems on the first visit, which could also give a distorted picture of the quality of nursing-home care available in the state. He also rejects a plan to use systematic sampling because once staff recognized the sampling ratio used they might be able to anticipate which nursing homes would be scheduled next for spot-checking. This would give staff an opportunity to give advance warning to nursing homes that were going to be remonitored. Moreover, a complete alphabetic list of nursing homes might be available to nursing-home administrators. They might easily be able to identify the sampling pattern in a systematic sampling and be able to anticipate which facilities were to be spot-checked next.

Consequently, the administrator decides to use a simple random sample of nursing homes for remonitoring. This system will make it impossible for staff or nursing-home administrators to anticipate which nursing homes will be checked next. Each nursing home in the target population will stand an equal chance of being monitored a second time, and the order in which the spot-checking will take place will be completely random.

3. Selecting a Sample Size

The resources available for this monitoring program allow for a 10 percent sample of nursing homes. In other words, sufficient money and staff resources are available to monitor 360 nursing homes a second time each year.

4. Listing the Target Population

The administrator has available to him an alphabetic list of all licensed and operating nursing homes in the state. He numbers these from 0001 to 3600.

5. Selecting the Sample Population

Closing his eyes to choose a random starting point in a table of random numbers, the administrator then reads down four-digit columns of random numbers until he has listed 360. In doing so, he rejects random numbers that exceed 3,600. Numbers that repeat themselves are only used once. The numbers chosen correspond to the identification numbers of the nursing-home facilities that are to be monitored a second time. It is important, however, that they be spot-checked *in the order in which they were chosen* rather than in alphabetic order. This eliminates the risk that nursing-home administrators or staff will anticipate the time of a possible spot check on the basis of their location in the alphabetic list. Staff will be informed about which facilities are to be spot-checked the day before visits are to be made. This will enable staff to plan their next day and inform the facility of the visit but will not provide an opportunity for nursing-home administrators to misrepresent the quality of care provided.

6. Checking the Representativeness of the Sample

A major concern of the administrator is whether public and private nursing-home facilities are adequately represented in the sample. In the target population of 3,600 nursing homes, approximately 33 percent are state operated and 67 percent are privately owned and operated. In the sample of 360, however, 36 percent are public and 64 percent are private. Since the percentages in sample and target populations do not match, he needs to know whether the sample population is representative of the target population and whether safe inferences can be made from the former to the latter. Using the formula set forth earlier in this chapter, he computes chi-square based on the differences between the observed frequencies for the sample population and the frequencies expected in a perfect representative sample. If the value of the chi-square exceeds 3.84, the differences between expected and observed populations will be too great to assume representativeness. In this case, it will mean that state-operated homes are overrepresented and privately-operated homes are underrepresented in the sample population, and that adjustments will have to be made in the inferences drawn from the sample population. More specifically, if state-run homes tended to provide higher-quality services and they were overrepresented in the sample population, then it would follow that conditions in nursing homes in the target population would be somewhat worse than those found in the sample population. If, on the other hand, conditions in private nursing homes were better and these homes were underrepresented, it would follow that nursing-home quality throughout the state was somewhat better than revealed in the sample population. Since the computed value of the chi-square is only 1.25, the administrator can assume that insofar as state versus private ownership is concerned, the sample population is representative.

He can then go on to test the representativeness of the sample population on other dimensions on which he has full knowledge of the target population, for example, program size, religious affiliation, level of training of staff. For each of these, he would compute the chi-square to assess the similarity between the target and sample populations. He would do this, however, only for the dimensions that he feels might be related to the quality of service rendered by these facilities.

EXERCISE

Select a target population of 1,000 agency clients. Draw an accidental sample of the first 100, a 10 percent systematic sample, and a 10 percent simple random sample. Compare the proportions of white and nonwhite clients in the target population with each of the three samples. For each sampling strategy, compute the chi-square based on the differences between the target population and the sample population. Which sampling strategy has produced the most representative sample?

SELECTED BIBLIOGRAPHY

Labovitz, Sanford, and Robert Hagedorn. *Introduction to Social Research*. New York: McGraw-Hill, 1971; pp. 28–35.

Levine, Samuel, and Freeman F. Elzey. *A Programmed Introduction to Research*. Belmont, Cal.: Wadsworth, 1968; pp. 70–96.

Netter, John. "How Accountants Save Money by Sampling," in J. M. Tanur, et al., eds., *Statistics: A Guide to the Unknown*. San Francisco: Holden-Day, 1972; pp. 203–11.

Stephen, Frederick J., and Philip J. McCarthy. *Sampling Opinions*. New York: John Wiley and Sons, 1963; pp. 3–122.

Walker, Helen M., and Joseph Lev. *Statistical Inference*. New York: Henry Holt, 1953; pp. 261–88.

CHAPTER NINE

Data Analysis and Interpretation for Program Monitoring

IF THEY ARE to be useful in program administration, program data must be properly analyzed and interpreted. Procedures for doing so involve techniques for summarizing, manipulating, and analyzing data economically and in such a way that appropriate inferences can be drawn from findings. These procedures rely on concepts from statistics, measurement theory, and information processing.

In this chapter, some concepts and techniques derived from these areas are applied to the processing of relatively simple and straightforward monitoring data. More specifically, the chapter concerns itself with the analysis and interpretation of "compliance data," that is, data that are collected to determine whether a program complies with predesignated personnel policies. Three sets of procedures are presented for analyzing and interpreting these data: first, the use of whole numbers, averages, and dispersions; second, the use of proportions; and third, the use of cross-tabulations. For each, a set of principles is articulated and examples are presented. The chi-square statistic is reintroduced, this time to determine whether observed agency practices are in accordance with or significantly different from predesignated personnel policies. Although our examples in this chapter deal almost exclusively with salary structure, the same principles may be used for analyzing hiring, promotion, and other personnel practices. Moreover, the analysis of compliance data can relate as well to the degree to which patterns of service delivery data are consistent with program policies.

DATA ANALYSIS AND INTERPRETATION FOR SOCIAL PROGRAM ADMINISTRATION

Data analysis and interpretation are essential to all types of research and useful in all areas of social program administration. In program planning, for example, a need survey or a resource interview is useful only when the data collected are appropriately manipulated, summarized, and understood. In program monitoring, compliance data are only useful if they are properly analyzed. If not, false assertions of compliance or noncompliance can be made. Finally, program evaluation efforts can generate enormous quantities of data. These data, however, are not ends in themselves. Rather they should be means for accurately assessing the impact of program interventions. This requires the distillation, analysis, and interpretation of the data so that correct inferences can be made about program efficiency and effectiveness.

PRINCIPLES FOR USING WHOLE NUMBERS, AVERAGES, AND DISPERSIONS

1. Computing a Frequency Distribution

The simplest kind of data available to a researcher is the frequency of units, observations, or individuals falling within each category of a single variable or dimension. If, for example, an administrator were interested in studying the salary structure of his organization, he would begin by determining how many employees in the organization fall into each salary category. From personnel files, he would then list each employee's salary. These data could then be presented in the form of a *simple frequency distribution* in which the numbers of individuals within each income category are indicated. The frequency distribution would look something like this:

Annual Salary	*Number of Employees*
$7,500	3
7,750	1
8,000	4
8,250	3
8,500	5
8,750	2

Annual Salary	Number of Employees
9,000	1
.....	.
.....	.
.....	<u>.</u>

Total Number of Employees $= N$

If individual salaries varied considerably and by small amounts, and a simple frequency distribution were too cumbersome, he might present the data in the form of a *grouped frequency distribution*. Here, salary levels are grouped in a manner that does not distort the basic frequency distribution, and the numbers of individuals falling within each *salary interval* are listed. A grouped frequency distribution would look something like this:

Annual Salary	Number of Employees
$ 7,001 to 8,000	8
8,001 to 9,000	11
9,001 to 10,000	15
10,001 to 11,000	10
....	<u>..</u>

Total Number of Employees $= N$

For purposes of presentation, grouped frequency distributions can be converted easily into *bar graphs* or *frequency polygons*. In both, salary intervals are plotted along a horizontal axis, with frequencies in each income interval plotted along a vertical axis. In the bar graph (figure 9.1) the width of each bar corresponds to each salary interval, and the height of each bar indicates the number of individuals within that interval.

Figure 9.1

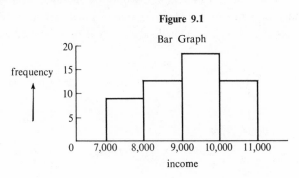

Figure 9.2

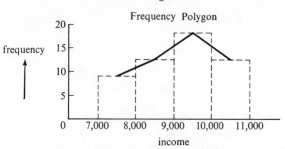

Frequency Polygon

In the frequency polygon (figure 9.2), the numbers of individuals within each salary interval are plotted along the vertical axis at the midpoint of each salary interval. The points are then connected with straight lines to give a graphic representation of the frequency distribution.

2. Choosing a Measure of Central Tendency

Once the frequency distribution has been specified, the data can be conveniently summarized in the form of a measure of central tendency or, in more common parlance, an average. Social researchers make use of three different measures of central tendency: the arithmetic mean, the median, and the mode. Each has its own advantages and disadvantages. Each offers a way to make an efficient summary statement about the data contained within the frequency distribution.

The *arithmetic mean* $(\overline{X})$ or the *arithmetic average* is the most widely known measure of central tendency. It is computed from the frequency distribution by taking the frequency within each interval, multiplying it by the value assigned to each interval, and dividing by the total number of units, observations, or individuals. Thus, if our original frequency distribution stopped at \$9,000, the mean annual salary would be computed as follows:

Annual Salary	Number of Employees	Salary × Number of Employees
\$7,500	3	\$22,500
7,750	1	7,750
8,000	4	32,000
8,250	3	24,750
8,500	5	42,500

Annual Salary	Number of Employees	Salary × Number of Employees
8,750	2	17,500
9,000	1	9,000
	Total = 19	Total = $156,000

$$\overline{X} = \frac{\$156,000}{19}$$

$$\overline{X} = \$8,211$$

Dividing the sum of the values of the salary intervals multiplied by the number of individuals in each category ($156,000) by the total number of employees (19) we arrive at the mean annual salary ($8,211).

Although the arithmetic mean is widely used and does give a good indication of the "average" annual salary within the foregoing population, it is likely to be distorted or skewed by extreme individual cases in the frequency distribution. Thus if a twentieth employee, the director of the above organization, were earning an annual salary of $30,000, the mean annual salary would be inflated to $9,300. If only the mean annual salary were reported, it would create the false impression that most employees' salaries hover around $9,300. However, our knowledge of the frequency distribution shows that, other than the director's, not one employee's salary even exceeds $9,000.

A second measure of central tendency is the median. The *median* is the point in the distribution that has the same number of scores (as close as possible to 50 percent) above and below it. In the preceding example, when the director's salary is not included, the median salary level would be $8,250, since 8 staff members have salaries below that figure and 8 above. The median is less precise than the mean. However, it is easier to compute and has the added advantage that it is not affected by extreme values the way the mean is. If we add the director's salary to the frequency distribution, the median remains $8,250. The median, therefore, gives a truer picture of the central tendency in frequency distributions that are skewed by extreme scores. As a consequence of its qualities the median is frequently used in table construction for dividing populations into low and high categories along a given dimension.

A third measure of central tendency is the *mode*. It is the category in the distribution that has the greatest number of scores. It is easiest to compute and least precise, and it is unaffected by extreme values. In the foregoing example, the mode is $8,500, since there are more employees in that category (5) than in any other. Note that, here again, the inclusion of the director's salary would not change the value.

In studies in which measures of central tendency are used, information about the values of these measures is frequently supplemented with information about the *dispersion* of the frequency distributions. This gives the reader a sense of the shape of the distributions and the degree to which they are skewed. Two common measures of dispersion are the range and the standard deviation. The *range* is simply the difference between the highest and lowest scores in the distribution. In the foregoing example, with the director's salary excluded, the range is $1,500. If the director's salary is included, the range would be $22,500.

The *standard deviation,* on the other hand, indicates the extent to which scores in the distributions cluster around the mean or are highly dispersed. The higher the standard deviation, the greater the dispersion from the mean.*

Whole numbers, averages, and dispersions are also useful for describing relationships between two or more variables. For example, one could describe the relationship between sex and annual salary by indicating the mean, median, or modal annual salary for male and female workers. To do this, one would plot the frequency distribution for each gender grouping. From the two frequency distributions, separate measures of central tendency would be computed for male and female workers.† In order to determine whether the two distributions are skewed, measures of dispersion would be computed for each group as well. This is particularly important because it would be possible to create a false impression of sex equality in salary levels by having a "token" female administrator with a high salary and presenting mean salary scores for each group. The female administrator's salary would elevate the mean salary score for women workers even though women may generally receive lower salaries than their male co-workers. Finally, if one wanted to "control" for effects of organizational status on the annual sal-

---

* For information about the computation of the standard deviation consult any basic statistical text.

† To determine the statistical significance of the differences between the two mean salaries, a statistical test called the t-test may be employed. Instructions for computing the t-test may be found in standard texts on statistical methods.

aries of men and women in the organization, one would compute the mean, median, or modal salaries of male and female line workers, supervisors, and administrators. For each of these sex and organizational status groups, one would plot the frequency distribution and compute the appropriate measures of central tendency and dispersion. A more meaningful comparison could then be made.

PRINCIPLES FOR USING PROPORTIONS AND CROSS-TABULATIONS

1. Analyzing Proportions and their Numerical Bases

The most common forms of data presentation are whole numbers or proportions. Each of these, *taken by itself,* can be extremely misleading. For example, two agencies may advertise themselves as "equal opportunity employers." Each report that they have hired 10 minority-group workers in the past year. On the face of it, they would appear equally open to minority employment. However, when we consider that 10 minority employees hired by program A constituted 50 percent of the total new employees of the program, and the 10 minority employees hired by program B constituted only 25 percent of the new employees hired by that program, then program A appears to be twice as open to minority employment as program B. Alternatively, two programs may report their minority hiring rates in percentages alone. Program A may indicate a 50 percent rate as compared with 25 percent for program B. Looking at the numerical bases upon which these percentages were computed, however, may reveal that one out of the two new employees hired in program A was from a minority group, as compared with 25 out of 100 new employees hired by program B. From the point of view of overall availability of jobs for minority persons, program B is 25 times as "open" as program A.

The point of this discussion is that *in presenting agency data, the proportions as well as the numbers upon which they were based should be clearly indicated.*

2. Analyzing Cross-Tabulations

Cross-tabulations are simple devices for analyzing and presenting relationships between two or more variables. They make use of whole numbers as well as proportions. However, for any single set of numerical cross-tabulations percentages can be taken in three different ways: vertically, horizontally, or against the total number in the table as a base. Each reveals a different aspect of the relationship between the two variables. Take, for example, the following numerical cross-tabulation of sex and annual salary among line workers in an organization. Using the median salary as the basis for dividing the population into two salary groupings and then determining the sex of the workers in each grouping, we come up with the following cross-tabulation:

	Male	Female	Total
$8,250 or less	100	200	300
More than $8,250	50	20	70
Total =	150	220	370

If this table were converted to percentages determined *vertically,* it would indicate the percentage of men and women workers in each annual salary category. Such a table would be most relevant to an analysis of sex bias in the organizational salary structure. It would look like this:

	Male	Female
$8,250 or less	67%	91%
More than $8,250	33%	8%
Total =	100%	100%

The table indicates that in the organization, 33 percent of the men earn over $8,250 annually as compared with only 8 percent of the women.

A table that used *horizontally* determined percentages would tell us the percentages in each annual salary category that were male or female, and which sex predominated in each of the income categories. The table would look like this:

	Male	Female	Total
$8,250 or less	33%	67%	100%
More than $8,250	71%	29%	100%

This table tells us that of those employees earning over $8,250, 71 percent are men. Of those earning $8,250 or less, 67 percent are women.

A third way of percentaging is against the total number of line workers as the numerical base. Such a table would describe the percentage of all line workers within each sex and annual salary category. It would look like this:

	Male	Female
$8,250 or less	27%	54%
More than $8,250	14%	5%
		100% = Total

This table indicates that out of the total organizational staff, 54 percent are women earning under $8,250, 27 percent are men earning under $8,250, 14 percent are men earning more than $8,250 and only 5 percent are women earning more than $8,250.

Each of these percentage tables reveals a different aspect of the relationship between sex and income within the organization. However, all the tables were derived from the same set of whole numbers.

Finally, using the original cross-tabulation of whole numbers, we can compute the chi-square statistic to determine whether the relationship found between sex and salary was likely to be the consequence of chance alone or the result of a real, possibly sexist pattern in the agency's salary structure. To do this, we must first calculate the expected number of males and females in each salary category under "ideal," totally equitable conditions. The formula for calculating these expected frequencies takes the proportion of each sex grouping in the total population and multiplies it by the total number of employees in that income category. So, for example, to compute the expected number of males earning under $8,250 one would use the following formula:

$$\frac{\text{Total males}}{\text{Total workers}} \times \text{Total workers under } \$8,250$$

The numbers taken from the original cross-tabulation are substituted, and the expected number of male workers earning less than $8,250 is found to be:

$$\frac{150}{370} \times 300 = 121.6$$

Following similar procedures, one can calculate the expected numbers for each cell in the original table. The following table indicates the observed and expected frequencies for each sex and salary category. The expected frequencies appear in parentheses.

	Male	Female
$8,250 or less	100 (121.6)	200 (178.4)
More than $8,250	50 (28.4)	20 (41.6)

The final computation of the chi-square involves adding the sum total of the squares of the differences between all pairs of observed and expected frequencies, divided by the expected frequencies for each pair. This is expressed as a formula, using the summation sign (Σ):

$$\chi^2 = \sum \frac{(O-E)^2}{E}$$

Substituting the numerical values from our expected and observed population of workers for the letters in the formula, we get:

$$\chi^2 = \frac{(100-121.6)^2}{(121.6)} + \frac{(200-178.4)^2}{(178.4)} + \frac{(50-28.4)^2}{(28.4)} + \frac{(20-41.6)^2}{(41.6)}$$

$$\chi^2 = 3.84 + 2.62 + 16.43 + 11.22$$

$$\chi^2 = 34.11$$

With a table of these proportions, a chi-square with any value less than 3.84 is generally taken to indicate that the observed population is not significantly different from the population expected under "ideal" conditions. Since the value of our chi-square (34.11) far exceeds the 3.84 criterion, we would then conclude that the observed differences between men's and women's salaries are not the product of chance variations in the data.* The next task is to discover whether these patterns reveal a "sexist" salary structure.

3. Controlling for Intervening Variables

The cross-tabulations presented above seem to reveal an organizational salary structure that discriminates against women. However, it would be premature to assert on the basis of these tables alone that there is a pattern of "institutional sexism," if we define this term as unequal pay for the same work. The relationship between gender and salary may be a consequence of some "legitimate" third factor that explains why women earn less than

---

* A chi-square greater than 3.84 is likely to occur less than five times in one hundred chances for a table of these proportions.

men. For example, it may turn out that women, by and large, have less previous experience than men. Since the salary structure of the organization compensates for previous experience, the differences between men and women may simply be a function of previous experience rather than of sex bias. Other factors such as length of tenure within the organization, prior education, and performance should be considered also. Researchers do this by computing cross-tabulations that "control" for these possibly "intervening" factors. This step routinely follows the computation of the cross-tabulation between the two variables with which one is primarily concerned.

We have established the fact that among the line workers in the organization men get paid more than women. Controlling for previous experience would require the construction of at least two additional tables, one comparing the annual salaries of men and women with no previous experience, and the other comparing the salaries of men and women with previous experience. If three previous-experience categories were employed, then three tables comparing men's and women's salaries would be constructed. Should the differences between men's and women's salaries persist in each of these tables, they would indicate that the original differences found in the first cross-tabulation could not be a consequence of differences in previous experience. This would lend support to the assertion that the organizational salary structure was sexist. These tables would look something like this:

	No Experience		Some Experience	
	Male	Female	Male	Female
$8,250 or less	75%	98%	50%	75%
More than $8,250	25%	2%	50%	25%

The tables above indicate that men and women do earn more when they have previous experience. We determine this by comparing the differences *between* experience categories *within* sex categories. Thus, 50 percent of the men with previous experience earn over $8,250 compared with only 25 percent of the men without previous experience. Likewise, for the women, 25 percent of the women with previous experience earn over $8,250, compared with only 2 percent of the women with no previous experience. For each group then there is about a 25 percent difference in salary level between those who do and those who do not have previous work experience.

However, when we "hold previous experience constant" and look at sex differences *within* experience categories, we see that among experienced workers, 50 percent of the men earn over \$8,250 as compared with only 25 percent of the experienced women. Looking at workers without previous experience, 25 percent of the men earn over \$8,250 as compared with only 2 percent of the inexperienced women. Thus, when previous experience is held constant, the percentage difference between men and women workers that we found in our original cross-tabulation persists. This means that the original differences found between men's and women's salaries cannot be attributed to differences in previous work experience.

If, on the other hand, we controlled for previous experience and our cross-tabulations looked like this:

	No Experience		Some Experience	
	Male	Female	Male	Female
\$8,250 or less	98%	98%	75%	75%
More than \$8,250	2%	2%	25%	25%

they would indicate that when previous experience is held constant, the original differences in men's and women's salaries disappear. The tables above indicate that experienced men and women do receive higher salaries than those without previous experience. However, *within* experience categories, men and women receive the same pay. Consequently, our original finding of a discrepancy between the annual salaries of male and female workers is "explained" not by institutional sexism, but by the fact that men in this organization tend to be more experienced workers than women. Here again a chi-square can be computed for each table to determine whether the patterns within are likely to be products of chance variations alone.

In general, it is extremely important to control for as many possible intervening variables as one can to determine the true explanation for a given finding. Assertions of institutional sexism, racism, and the like are premature without the exercise of such controls.

Hypothetical Illustration

An agency administrator is concerned about maintaining personnel practices that are equitable and in compliance with "affirmative action" guidelines. Recently, however, charges of "reverse racism" have been made by nonminority staff who contend that minority-group supervisors get paid more for the same jobs in the agency. The administrator's task is to collect and analyze the data relevant to this issue and to interpret the findings to staff. Should the data reveal salary inequities of any kind, the administrator would take measures to correct these.

COLLECTING AND ANALYZING THE DATA

In order to collect the relevant data, the administrator requests that the agency's personnel officer turn over to him all the data concerning each supervisor's minority or nonminority status and any other data that might legitimately influence salary level, e.g., performance measures, extent of previous experience, prior education, scores on qualifying examinations for the position, tenure within the organization, and so on.

1. Computing a Salary Distribution and Measures of Central Tendency

The administrator begins the data analysis by computing a salary distribution for all supervisors. This involves listing each salary category and the number of supervisors whose salaries fall within it. On the basis of the resulting frequency distribution, the administrator calculates the mean and the median salaries for all supervisors within the agency. He determines that the mean salary for all supervisors is $11,383 per year, with the median slightly higher at $11,400. He then computes a frequency distribution separately for minority and nonminority supervisors. Doing this, he finds that, indeed, minority-group supervisors enjoy higher mean and median salaries than do nonminority supervisors. Minority-group supervisors, for example, receive a mean salary of $11,842 as contrasted with a mean salary of $11,095 for nonminority supervisors.

These data on the face of it seem to support the contention that minority-group supervisors receive preferential treatment. They *do* receive higher pay for the same work.

2. Computing Cross-Tabulations and the Chi-Square

Using the median salary earned by all supervisors ($11,400) as a "cut-off point" for dividing the supervisors by salary, the administrator then specifies a cross-tabulation between minority and nonminority status and salary. This table indicates the number of minority and nonminority supervisors earning salaries below and above the median salary for the total population

of supervisors. Computing the chi-square for the cross-tabulation reveals
that the difference in median salary between minority and nonminority supervisors is greater than one would expect to find from chance variations.
His next task is to discover whether these patterns indicate a salary structure
that favors minority-group supervisors.

3. Controlling for Intervening Variables

To determine whether minority-group supervisors do receive preferential
treatment in salary decisions, he computes a series of tables indicating the
relationship between minority-group status and salary, controlling for possible intervening variables such as performance measures and prior education.
Holding performance levels constant, he finds that minority-group supervisors still have significantly higher salaries than nonminority-group supervisors who perform equally well. The difference also persists when prior education is controlled. However, controlling for the variable "years of
previous experience," he finds that the difference between minority and
nonminority supervisors no longer exists. The reason for the original differences between supervisors' salaries was that minority-group supervisors
tended to have significantly more previous work experience, which is considered a legitimate element in the computation of salary increments. Hence,
it is concluded on the basis of these data that there is no evidence of discrim-
inatory personnel practices. These findings are then communicated to staff.
No change in personnel practice is recommended.

EXERCISE

Select an agency that will provide you with descriptive data on clients' incomes, types of problem presented, and whether or not clients were accepted for service. Compute the frequency distribution for clients' incomes
and the mean, median, and modal income of the total client population.
Using the median income for dividing income categories, construct a table
cross-tabulating client income and acceptance for agency service. Compute
the percentages of each client-income group accepted or rejected. Does any
pattern emerge? Compute a chi-square to determine whether there is a statistically significant relationship between these two variables. Finally, construct a set of tables controlling for the effects of problem type. Interpret the

findings. Does the problem type "explain" any of the original differences found in the acceptance rates of lower and higher income clients?

SELECTED BIBLIOGRAPHY

Amos, Jimmy R., Foster L. Brown, and Oscar G. Mink. *Statistical Concepts: A Basic Program.* New York: Harper and Row, 1965; 125 pp.

Goldstein, Harris K. *Research Standards and Methods for Social Workers.* New Orleans, La.: The Hauser Press, 1963; pp. 179–295.

Hirschi, Travis, and Hanan C. Selvin. *Delinquency Research.* New York: The Free Press, 1967; pp. 35–142.

Huff, Darrell. *How to Lie With Statistics.* New York: W. W. Norton, 1954; 142 pp.

Wallis, W. Allen, and Harry Roberts. *The Nature of Statistics.* New York: The Free Press, 1965; pp. 89–122, 177–207.

Weiss, Robert S. *Statistics in Social Research.* New York: John Wiley and Sons, 1968; pp. 244–75.

PART THREE

PROGRAM EVALUATION

PROGRAM EVALUATION is the process by which program effectiveness and efficiency are assessed. It involves the collection, analysis, and interpretation of data bearing on the achievement of program goals, in contrast to program monitoring, which considers the extent to which program operations follow specifications. For example, monitoring tells us whether a tutorial reading program has sufficient staff and technical resources, has successfully recruited the designated client population, and is faithfully implementing the program's strategy for teaching reading skills. Evaluation tells us whether the children who participated in the program did, in fact, improve their reading skills (that is, the program's effectiveness) and at what cost (its efficiency).

Effectiveness considers questions like: how successful has a vocational rehabilitation program been in securing and sustaining job placements for program clientele; how successful has a social hygiene program been in reducing the incidence of venereal disease within a specified target population; how successful has a community coordination council been in coordinating social services within a given community and in reducing unnecessary duplication of services; how successful has a child-abuse program been in reducing incidents of child abuse; and so on.

Program *efficiency* is concerned with the costs, in money, time, staff resources, and so on, of achieving these goals. In other words, program efficiency is the ratio of program effectiveness to program efforts. This concept makes possible the evaluation of the relative costs of different program strategies to achieve the same goal. As such, it is extremely useful for administrative decision making.

Although both are essential aspects of program evaluation, effectiveness and efficiency do not always go together. In fact, some programs are quite effective but require great sums of time, money, and staff input. Others are highly efficient but are limited in their accomplishments. Sad to say, some programs are neither effective nor efficient and should be scrapped. Ideally, of course, a responsible administrator attempts to maximize both effectiveness and efficiency through program evaluation.

Evaluation can also provide information that is meant to be generalized to other, comparable programs and situations. We refer to this as *summative evaluation*. By contrast, program evaluation which is mainly concerned with assessing and improving a specific program, without regard to the generalizability of the findings, is called *formative evaluation*.*

ADMINISTRATIVE DECISIONS IN PROGRAM EVALUATION

Perhaps the most important decision an administrator must make relative to evaluation is whether to conduct a summative or a formative evaluation. To conduct a summative evaluation, a "classical experimental model" is typically employed. This means that a target population is specified and a representative sample is selected through probability sampling techniques. The sample population is then allocated randomly into at least one experimental group, which receives a specified and highly standardized program intervention, and at least one control group, which receives either no intervention or a placebo. "Baseline" measurements, or measurements prior to intervention, are taken on both experimental and control groups. Similar measurements are taken after intervention to determine whether changes have taken place that can be causally attributed to the program intervention.

This model is very costly and usually requires research and statistical consultation. It also raises many technical, practical, and ethical problems for administrators, evaluators, and program staff. When used properly, it can contribute significantly to our general understanding of program policy and its impact. However, it is often of little use to program administrators, who are, appropriately, more concerned with their own programs than with producing generalizable knowledge; who must make program decisions *during* the operation of a program rather than *after* all the clients have been served; and who do not have the technical or material resources to implement such a

---

* For a more detailed discussion of the distinction between summative and formative evaluation, *see* Scriven, "Methodology of Evaluation."

study. Not surprisingly, however, research consultants generally recommend summative evaluation designs.

In formative evaluations, program objectives and interventions are specified and translated into measurable indices. Then data concerning program means and ends are collected and analyzed within the context of a relatively simple, logical design.

Formative evaluations do not generate knowledge that can easily be applied to other programs. They make possible inferences which are only suggestive of cause-effect relationships because they do not routinely employ control groups or random allocation of subjects. Knowledge about the relationship between program interventions and client outcomes is thus purely "correlational." Formative evaluations can provide the impetus for subsequent summative evaluation. However, the major advantages of formative evaluations are that they are less costly, require less expertise, present fewer practical and ethical problems, and provide more immediate feedback of results than do summative evaluations.

Other decisions that must be made in planning for program evaluation involve the relative importance of effectiveness versus efficiency measures in assessing the impact of program operations, who will conduct the evaluation, and the extent and type of staff involvement in the evaluation process. These decisions are beyond the scope of this book.*

The information generated by program evaluation can, in turn, contribute to administrative decision making about the expansion, contraction, and/or modification of existing social programs. Such information provides a rational basis for decisions about service delivery, staff allocation, intervention strategies, budgetary priorities, and so on.

RESEARCH TECHNIQUES AND FORMATIVE EVALUATION

Elsewhere, we have discussed evaluation strategies that either rely heavily on research consultation or require full-time research staff for their implementation.† In this book, however, our emphasis is on administrative self-evaluation with minimal reliance on research consultation or permanent research staff. It is assumed that administrators are able to secure staff involvement and to reduce possible staff-administrator conflicts that could un-

* For a discussion of some of these issues, see Tripoli, Fellin, and Epstein, *Social Program Evaluation*.
† Ibid.

dermine their efforts at formative evaluation. The next four chapters are limited to formative evaluation strategies that are logical constructs for making inferences about program effectiveness and efficiency. They make use of the data-collection and data-analytic techniques discussed in previous chapters in this book.

In chapter 10, for example, we discuss the interrupted time series design, a strategy making use of a series of measurements taken before and after program intervention. It is a basic design for providing correlational information about program interventions and outcomes.

Chapter 11 introduces the replicated cross-sectional survey design. This procedure can provide almost immediate feedback of information about the effects and efficiency of client processing in continuous programs in which clients move through a predictable set of stages or statuses.

Comparative designs are discussed in chapter 12. They are used for comparing two or more program interventions and for making judgments about their relative effectiveness and efficiency.

Finally, in chapter 13, we discuss the crossover design. This can be used in programs that have large numbers of applicants, long waiting lists, and limited program vacancies and that involve a relatively short period of contact with clientele.

This is by no means an exhaustive listing of formative evaluation strategies. We have selected those that we believe will be most useful to program administrators who want to conduct their own formative evaluations. Moreover, since we are limiting ourselves to social research techniques, benefit-cost analysis and other cost-analytic techniques that are frequently used in assessing program efficiency will not be discussed.

SELECTED BIBLIOGRAPHY

Freeman, Howard E., and Clarence C. Sherwood, *Social Research and Social Policy*. Englewood Cliffs, N.J.: Prentice-Hall, 1970; pp. 70–83.

Riecken, H. W., and R. F. Boruch, eds. *Social Experimentation*. New York: Academic Press, 1974; pp. 1–13.

Rossi, P. H., and W. Williams, eds. *Evaluating Social Programs*. New York: Seminar Press, 1972; pp. 5–49.

Scriven, M. "The Methodology of Evaluation," in R. W. Tyler, R. M. Gagne, and M. Scriven, eds., *Perspectives of Curriculum Evaluation*. AERA Monograph

Series on Curriculum Evaluation, no. 1. Chicago: Rand McNally, 1967; pp. 39–83.

Suchman, E. A. *Evaluative Research*. New York: Russell Sage Foundation, 1967; pp. 27–50.

Tripodi, Tony, Phillip Fellin, and Irwin Epstein. *Social Program Evaluation*. Itasca, Ill.: F. E. Peacock, 1971; pp. 41–60.

Weiss, Carol H. *Evaluation Research*. Englewood Cliffs, N.J.: Prentice-Hall, 1972; pp. 1–23.

CHAPTER TEN

Interrupted Time Series Designs

AT BEST, formative evaluation designs are only quasi-experiments, since they rarely employ randomization procedures or experimental and control groups and the knowledge they produce is only suggestive of causality. Consequently, formative evaluations are not affected by problems of external validity, that is, the extent to which inferences can be made to other populations and settings.

Formative evaluations *are* seriously affected by problems of *internal validity,* that is, the extent to which it can be inferred that: program interventions do affect particular outcomes; evaluation instruments do accurately describe and measure interventions and outcomes; and the evaluation process itself does not influence program outcomes.

In their classic monograph "Experimental and Quasi-Experimental Designs for Research," Campbell and Stanley identify eight factors that can jeopardize the internal validity of inferences drawn from a study. Applied to the area of program evaluation, these are: (1) contemporary history—unanticipated events may occur while a program is under way that change the character of the intervention, the client's situation, or the client himself; (2) maturation—during the course of program intervention clients may change simply as a function of time, developmental growth, fatigue, and so on; (3) initial measurement effects—the process of measurement itself might affect client outcomes; (4) instrumentation—unreliability over time due to lack of standardization of the measure; (5) statistical regression, the tendency of research groups selected for intervention on the basis of extreme scores on some index of need or pathology to "naturally" regress to a more average score in subsequent testing regardless of the effects of program interventions; (6) selection—differences between experimental and control groups, or among groups receiving different kinds of interventions, can yield misleading findings; (7) subject mortality—certain types of subjects may drop out of the program in disproportionate numbers, creating misleading findings; and (8) interaction effects—the combined effects of any and all of the above factors may be mistaken for the effects of program interventions.

Unfortunately, two of the designs most frequently used by administrators in formative evaluations do not take adequate account of these threats to internal validity. The first, the *after-only* design, attempts to measure the results of program intervention after it has taken place. No data are collected before, and there is only one measurement taken after program intervention. As a result, it is impossible to determine whether the findings of such a study reveal true differences in program recipients that are consequences of the program intervention and that are stable over time.

A second, commonly used formative evaluation design is the *pretest/post-test* design. In this approach, one measurement is taken before and one after program intervention. Changes in client scores are attributed to program intervention. While this design is an improvement over the after-only design, measurement differences are as likely to be the result of measurement instability as of program intervention.

The design that controls for measurement instability both before and after program intervention is the *interrupted time series* design. In this design, a series of measurements are made before program intervention on variables that program intends to influence. These measurements serve as a *baseline* against which postintervention measurements are compared. A series of measurements is made after program intervention begins, to determine whether changes attributed to the program are stable over time.

Although the interrupted time series design does not control for *all* factors affecting internal validity, does not produce knowledge that is clearly and undisputably causal, and does not produce findings that are generalizeable to other programs, it does generate knowledge that is highly informative about a specific program.

In addition, the basic interrupted time series design can be embellished through the use of randomly assigned comparison or control groups that receive different interventions or no interventions at all. Finally, randomly assigned comparison groups may receive the same intervention at different points in time. This *time-lag* design controls for the effects of contemporary history. Within each group, however, the same series of measurements is taken before and after program intervention. Comparisons are made within and between the groups to gauge more precisely the impact of program intervention.

INTERRUPTED TIME SERIES DESIGNS AND SOCIAL PROGRAM ADMINISTRATION

Interrupted time series designs are used mainly to study the effectiveness of program efforts. The data for such studies may be taken from agency archives. For example, schools routinely keep records on attendance, grades, disciplinary actions for all students. Social agency case records often contain repeated indications of a client's social, psychological, and economic situation. These archival data can serve as a basis for a series of measurements before and after specific program interventions begin.

In programs that do not routinely collect such data, original data may be generated through the use of forms, observational techniques, questionnaires, interviews, and so on. These techniques were discussed more fully in previous chapters.

PRINCIPLES FOR IMPLEMENTING THE INTERRUPTED TIME SERIES DESIGN

1. Identifying Program Objectives

Program objectives are the ends to which program efforts are directed. To evaluate the effectiveness of a program one must first describe these objectives in specific, concrete terms.

Program goals may be stated, generally in program proposals and other agency documents. A simple device for translating abstract goals into specific objectives is to identify *who* in the program (which agency personnel) are expected to do *what* (using what procedures, strategies, therapeutic approaches, provision of services, etc.) to *whom* (the designated target population) *where* (at what location), *when* (with what frequency), and *why* (to accomplish what ends or objectives)? Once these questions are answered, measures can be developed for determining the extent to which objectives are, in fact, achieved.

2. Operationally Defining Program Objectives

Once program objectives are stated in concrete terms, they can be *operationally defined,* that is, converted into measurable scales. These scales may be nominal, ordinal, interval, or ratio scales and should be subjected to tests of measurement reliability and validity (see chapter 4). *For an interrupted time series design, it is especially important that measures of effectiveness have a high test/retest reliability* (for example, a correlation of at least .80) since the research design requires repeated use of the same measures. If test/retest reliability is low, it is impossible to determine whether fluctuation in effectiveness measurements is an indicator of the impact of the program or of the instability of the measuring device.

There are several possible sources of data for measuring effectiveness. Gottman and Leiblum * suggest the use of archival data, frequency counts through direct observation, client ratings, and postprogram evaluation sheets filled out by clients and/or staff. For client or staff ratings, either interviews or self-administered questionnaires may be used.

For example, in an adult corrections program, one of the specific goals may be to see to it that probationers maintain good job performance in some form of legitimate employment. More specifically, this refers to factors such as attendance, tardiness, quality and quantity of work performed, relationships with co-workers, and the like. Data bearing on these factors can be drawn from personnel records, direct observations, questionnaires filled out by work supervisors, interviews with or questionnaires administered to work supervisors, and questionnaires or interviews administered to probationers themselves. Each of these methods raises different issues of measurement reliability, validity, cost, and feasibility. However, they all can provide important information about probationers' job performance.

3. Specifying the Intervention Strategy

Once program objectives are identified and operationally defined, the means for achieving program objectives should be specified. A complete and behaviorally specific description of the intervention strategy is necessary to determine whether staff are, in fact, providing the intended intervention. Without this, it would be improper to infer that a particular intervention strategy was more or less effective. In other words, in order to test the effec-

---

* See Gottman and Leiblum, *How to Do Psychotherapy and How to Evaluate It.*

tiveness of a particular intervention strategy, one must first determine whether it is being implemented. Thus, if probation officers are supposed to be seeing their clients monthly, before the effectiveness of this service can be tested it must first be determined that workers are seeing their clients monthly. This may require some degree of program monitoring.

Specification of the intervention strategy is also important for implementing new programs based on previous effectiveness studies. A program may be proven to be effective, but if no one bothers to specify rigorously what staff did, the previous study is useless for shaping new programs.

4. Taking a Series of Baseline Measurements

Prior to the introduction of the program of intervention, a series of measurements should be taken on one or more variables selected for measuring effectiveness. These baseline measures should be taken at regular and appropriate intervals. For example, for classroom behavior, measurements may be taken on a daily basis. For parole violations, monthly measures may be appropriate. Here again, issues of cost and feasibility enter in. After intervention begins, the same time intervals will be used for determining program effectiveness.

It is also extremely important that measurement conditions be standardized and applied consistently for each baseline and postintervention measurement, to limit the possibility that fluctuations in the data are the consequence of different testing conditions.

Ideally, approximately 10 to 15 baseline measurements should be taken. This should insure a degree of stability in the time series.

5. Graphing the Baseline Data

To insure that a detectable degree of stability is established in the preintervention time series, baseline data should be represented on a separate graph for each effectiveness variable. The graph is a visual device for observing regularities in the data over time. In the graph, the horizontal axis is used to represent the time intervals between measurements. The vertical axis is used to represent either individual scores for one study subject or mean scores for more than one subject.

Stability is established when the line connecting the scores on a particular effectiveness measure: runs parallel to the horizontal axis of the graph (fig-

Figure 10.1

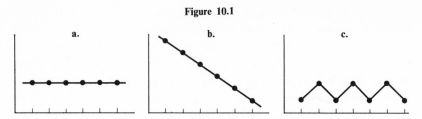

ure 10.1*a*); is not parallel, but maintains a constant angle or slope with relation to the horizontal axis (*b*); or follows a regular and consistent pattern (*c*).

6. Implementing the Program

Once a stable pattern is established in the baseline data, the program strategy should be immediately and fully introduced. Moreover, interventions
should be standardized so that every program participant receives the same
services and/or treatments. A study of a program implemented partially or
gradually is more likely to produce findings that are the consequence of
some extraneous factor such as maturation. A study of a program in which
intervention is not standardized is more likely to yield findings that are the
consequence of differences in patterns of intervention. Immediate, complete,
and standardized interventions allow for clearer interpretation of the effects
of the program.

7. Taking a Series of Post-Intervention Measurements

A series of postintervention measurements should be taken throughout the
intervention period, using the same time intervals, standardization procedures, and effectiveness measures employed in establishing a baseline. The
use of the same procedures reduces the chances that measured "effects" are
the product of random errors in the measurement process and increases the
chances that study findings truly reflect program outcomes. The data should
then be graphed alongside the baseline data. The point at which program intervention begins should be clearly discernible.*

8. Collecting Supportive Data Regarding Contemporary History

The interrupted time series design does not control for the effects of
contemporary history. However, it is possible to collect supportive evidence

---

* This type of pre- and postintervention graph is sometimes referred to as a "Shewart chart."

regarding the extent to which events external to the program might have influenced client outcomes. For example, clients may be interviewed to determine whether any critical changes occurred in their lives (for example, changes in economic status, family composition, physical health) that may have had an influence on the success or failure of program intervention. Although clients may not be totally aware of the effects of all extraneous variables on their lives, this procedure can be used to control for the effects of those major influences of which they are aware.

9. Comparing Pre- and Postintervention Patterns

After pre- and postintervention data have been graphed, the trend lines are compared visually. Is there a change in the magnitude of the observations after intervention (figure 10.2a)? Is there a change in the slope of the observations after intervention (b)? Is there a change in the pattern of the observations (c)?

If changes are discernible by visual inspection of the graph, one should seek confirmation that changes do not occur as a result of chance variations, but are statistically significant. One simple technique for determining whether differences are likely to be statistically significant has been proposed by Gottman; this technique is only useful however, when postinter-

Figure 10.2

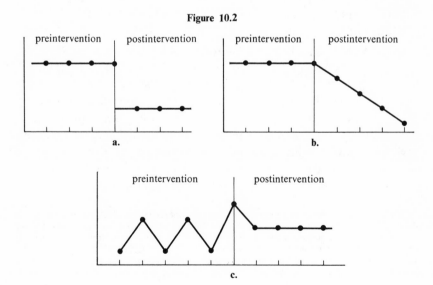

Figure 10.3

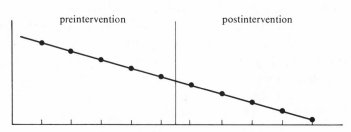

vention data do not represent a continuation of the same trend line established in the baseline measures.* For example, the findings in figure 10.3 could not be used since they would give an erroneous impression of statistical significance when, in fact, the ''effects'' are not the result of program intervention. Thus, an inspection of the trend line in figure 10.3 strongly suggests that the postintervention outcomes would have occurred without any intervention at all as a result of factors already operative during the preintervention phase.

To illustrate the process proposed by Gottman, consider the following example. A state Department of Corrections decides to implement a new group therapy program to reduce the number of parole violations committed by recently released criminal offenders. Figure 10.4 represents the pre- and postintervention data taken monthly over a period of a year.

Visual inspection of the data reveals a decline in the rate of parole violation after intervention. To determine whether this decline is likely to be statistically significant: (1) calculate the mean for the baseline data; (2) draw a line parallel to the horizontal axis representing the mean for the baseline data; (3) calculate the standard deviation for the baseline data; (4) multiply the standard deviation by 2; (5) add this figure to the mean; (6) subtract it from the mean; (7) draw lines parallel to the horizontal axis, two standard deviations above and below the mean. If the postintervention observations are found outside these lines, it strongly suggests that the postintervention changes are statistically significant at the .05 level of probability.

* Gottman and Leiblum, *How to Do Psychotherapy and How to Evaluate It*. The procedure suggested by Gottman also rested on the assumption that measurements taken at each interval are not influenced by previous measurements (that is, they are independent of each other) and that measurements are taken at randomly selected times. Since neither criterion is likely to be met in an interrupted time series study, our use of the Gottman procedure yields only an approximation to statistical significance.

Figure 10.4

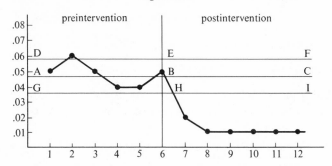

Following the foregoing instructions in our probation example, we calculate the arithmetic mean of the baseline data $(\bar{X})$ by taking the sum of the scores of the baseline observations and dividing by the total number of observation periods prior to intervention.

$$\bar{X} = \frac{.05 + .06 + .05 + .04 + .04 + .05}{6}$$

$$\bar{X} = .0483$$

Line ABC in figure 10.4 represents the mean of the baseline data.

To calculate the standard deviation (SD) of the baseline mean, we take the square root of the sum of the differences between each baseline observation and the baseline mean, square it and divide by the total number of baseline observations. Expressed as a formula, this is:

$$SD = \sqrt{\frac{\Sigma \ (\text{each observation} - \text{mean})^2}{N}}$$

Substituting our probation violation data in the formula, we get:

$$SD = \sqrt{\frac{\begin{array}{c}(.05 - .0483)^2 + (.06 - .0483)^2 + (.05 - .0483)^2 + \\ (.04 - .0483)^2 + (.04 - .0483)^2 + (.05 - .0483)^2\end{array}}{6}}$$

$$SD = .00553$$

We then multiply the standard deviation by 2:

$$2 \ SD = .111$$

Adding this to the mean gives us:

$.0483 + .0111 = .0594 = 2$ standard deviations above the mean.

Subtracting from the mean gives us:

$.0483 - .0111 = .0371 = 2$ standard deviations below the mean.

Line DEF in figure 10.4 represents the line two standard deviations above the mean. Line GHI in figure 10.4 represents the line two standard deviations below the mean.

Since all the postintervention observations in figure 10.4 fall below line GHI, the reduction in parole violations after intervention is likely to be statistically significant beyond the .05 level of probability. If the postintervention observations were above line DEF, this would probably indicate a statistically significant increase in parole violations after intervention. Finally, if most of the postintervention observations fell between DEF and GHI, this would indicate that the program had no statistically significant impact on parole violations.

Other, more complicated statistical techniques for analyzing interrupted time series data are suggested by Gottman and Leiblum and by Caporaso.* If the data do not lend themselves to visual interpretation and to the simple statistical technique described above, a research consultant might be required to employ more complicated tests of significance.

Hypothetical Illustration

PROBLEM SITUATION AND ADMINISTRATIVE TASK

Assembly line workers in a small factory are showing signs of increasing alienation. Absenteeism is high. Productivity is declining. Industrial accidents are increasing, and there is evidence that some workers are becoming dependent on drugs. Moreover, workers are increasingly expressing their dissatisfaction with the dull and monotonous nature of their work.

An enlightened management decides to introduce a program to reduce worker alienation and to increase productivity (efficiency and effectiveness). The program involves the creation of a workers' advisory group to advise management on problems with existing work conditions, the introduction of

* See Gottman and Leiblum, *How to Do Psychotherapy and How to Evaluate It;* Caporaso, "Quasi-Experimental Approaches."

a work incentive program through which workers can earn additional income through greater productivity and lower absenteeism, the introduction of a new policy that allows workers to go home or to attend classes when daily production quotas have been achieved, and the availability of free drug counseling for those workers who desire it or whose work has fallen off so badly that it is the only alternative to firing them.

IMPLEMENTING AN INTERRUPTED TIME SERIES DESIGN

1. Identifying Program Objectives

The program of intervention has two general objectives, the reduction of worker alienation and increased productivity. More specifically, the program aims to reduce absenteeism, increase positive work attitudes and sentiments, reduce accidents and reported illnesses on the job, reduce drug dependency, increase the number of units of output (effectiveness), and reduce the cost per unit of output produced (efficiency).

2. Operationally Defining Program Objectives

For these different dimensions of alienation and productivity, different measures must be constructed on the basis of data gathered in different ways. For example, measurements of absenteeism can be taken from data available from the company payroll office, which routinely monitors attendance. Attendance rates for assembly line workers can easily be calculated on a daily, weekly, or monthly basis. The intervals chosen, however, may differ from variable to variable depending on availability, feasibility, and the like.

Work attitudes can be measured by distributing an anonymous questionnaire to workers periodically. For example, a series of "Likert-scale" items may be given to workers at regular intervals in which they indicate their strong agreement, moderate agreement, moderate disagreement, or strong disagreement with statements such as:

The only good thing about work is getting paid.
I'd rather be home sick than come in to work.
I really like my job.

Strong agreement with the first two statements and strong disagreement with the third would indicate a high level of alienation. Average alienation scores could then be computed for all workers at periodic intervals. After pretesting, those items that yield a high test/retest reliability coefficient will be used to measure worker alienation.

The rates of industrial accidents can be computed from data routinely available from the company health and safety office. Here issues of measurement reliability and validity become somewhat problematic, since the degree of seriousness of accidents may have to be considered. In addition, illness reports will have to be distinguished from accident reports and analyzed separately. The possible linkage between illness and accident for those who are using drugs at work makes for some difficulty in distinguishing these two dimensions. Nevertheless, the numbers of daily, weekly, or monthly accident and illness complaints can easily be calculated.

For those workers who volunteer or who are required to participate in the drug counseling program, separate self-reported indexes of daily drug use can be constructed. However, these data should be supplemented by the use of pharmacological testing such as the analysis of daily urine samples. In order to assure the validity of this testing process, procedures must be developed to insure that workers submit their own urine samples for testing.

Finally, data on productivity should be routinely available from the company's research and development department, which collects data on the number of units produced weekly and on the costs of production.

3. Specifying the Intervention Strategy

Once the variables for measuring the impact of intervention have been operationalized, the intervention program should be fully described. This requires a complete description of the new worker's advisory program, the new work-incentive system, and the drug counseling program. For each program intervention, the questions who does what to whom where, when, and why should be answered. Ideally, program monitoring data should also be collected on the quantity and quality of staff and worker participation in each program. Although this would increase the cost of the study, it would also indicate which elements of the intervention are operating as planned and which are not.

4. Taking a Series of Baseline Measurements

To measure attendance, worker attitudes, industrial accidents and illnesses reported on the job, and productivity, a series of weekly measures is taken. After five weeks' testing, relatively stable baselines are established.

For those volunteering or required to participate in the drug counseling program, daily monitoring is necessary. This is begun after stable baselines are established on the other dimensions so that the program can be implemented as soon as a stable baseline is established for those with drug problems. This strategy minimizes the amount of time those on drugs will have to be monitored before receiving treatment.

5. Graphing the Baseline Data

For *each* measurement of program objectives, a *separate graph* is drawn indicating the slope of the baseline.

6. Implementing the Program

Management then announces the introduction of the full range of interventions. Social scientists would probably be inclined to want to introduce each of the interventions separately to determine the relative impact of each. However, management is, at this point, more interested in finding a solution to its production and personnel problems than in determining the relative impact of one or another program. In the future, if the cost of these programs becomes too great, questions of relative cost and/or effectiveness may become more salient to management.*

7. Taking a Series of Post-Intervention Measurements

Once the intervention program has been initiated, postintervention data are collected, using the data sources, data collection instruments, and time intervals used in collecting baseline data. These data are collected over a six-month period and graphed alongside the baseline data.

8. Collecting Supportive Data Regarding Contemporary History

Although a decision is taken not to collect data from *all* workers about the impact of factors external to the work situation on their performance, this information is collected from participants in the drug counseling program. Such information may be useful in determining whether family and interpersonal problems outside the plant are either reinforcing drug dependency or reducing the possibilities of cure.

---

* For designs that can be used to evaluate individual components within a program, see chapter 12 on comparative experimentation and chapter 13 on crossover designs.

9. Comparing Pre- and Postintervention Patterns

After the postintervention data have been collected, visual and statistical comparisons are made between pre- and postintervention patterns for each of the variables measured. The graphs indicate that although attendance and productivity are higher, and industrial accidents and reported illness are lower, worker attitudes remain fairly negative. Moreover, the drug program appears to be working, but only with those who voluntarily participate in the program. Supplementary data (on contemporary history) suggest that those who are required to participate have more serious and pervasive interpersonal problems, which require more extensive intervention than the program can provide. For the most part, however, the intervention appears to be successful. Additional programs to reduce worker alienation will be considered as well as possible resources for workers with drug problems that do not yield to the counseling available through the company-sponsored program.

EXERCISE

Devise an interrupted time series study design to evaluate a program designed to increase school attendance and grades and to decrease disruptive behaviors in a junior high school. Specify the measures to be used and the program to be implemented. How feasible is the program of intervention and the plan for evaluation? How likely is it to produce the desired results? What would these results look like if they were graphed?

SELECTED BIBLIOGRAPHY

Campbell, D. T. "Reforms as Experiments," in J. A. Caporaso and L. L. Roos, Jr., eds., *Quasi-Experimental Approaches*. Evanston, Ill.: Northwestern University Press, 1973; pp. 187–225.

Campbell, D. T., and J. C. Stanley. "Experimental and Quasi-Experimental Designs for Research," in N. L. Cage, ed., *Handbook of Educational Research*. New York: Rand McNally, 1963.

Caporaso, J. A. "Quasi-Experimental Approaches to Social Science: Perspectives and Problems," in J. A. Caporaso and L. L. Roos, Jr., eds., *Quasi-Experimental Approaches*. Evanston, Ill.: Northwestern University Press, 1973; pp. 3–38.

Gottman, J. M., and S. R. Leiblum. *How to Do Psychotherapy and How to Evaluate It*. New York: Holt, Rinehart, and Winston, 1974; pp. 47–63, 138–51.

Riecken, H. W., and R. F. Boruch, eds., *Social Experimentation*. New York: Academic Press, 1974; pp. 97–108.

CHAPTER ELEVEN

Replicated Cross-Sectional Survey Designs

INTERRUPTED TIME SERIES STUDIES, discussed in the previous chapter, begin *before* new programs, policies, or intervention strategies are implemented. They require a high level of administrative and technological control so that program interventions can be introduced fully and immediately after a stable baseline is established.

Often, however, programs that are already under way or programs in which there is a relatively low level of administrative and technological control require evaluation. Such progress can be evaluated through the replicated cross-sectional survey design.

The replicated cross-sectional survey design is a special use of survey methods. It can be used to gather information about perceptions, attitudes, beliefs, and behaviors of clients who are at different stages in program processing. Data are gathered through the administration of the same interview or questionnaire simultaneously to different samples of clients who are at different stages in the "normal" program cycle. The results are interpreted as reflecting the changes that a single client group experiences as a consequence of program processing.

For example, in a family service agency, samples of clients who are at the intake, treatment, and termination phases are interviewed. If sufficient resources are available, follow-up interviews may be conducted with a sample of clients weeks or months after treatment has been completed.

Typically, those chosen for interviewing at each program phase are selected through random sampling. Their responses are then tabulated, analyzed, compared, and interpreted. The results are then used to make inferences about the probable impact of the program on clients as a group as they move through various program stages. These studies do not provide cause-effect knowledge, nor do they provide information about program impact on individual clients. Their major advantage is that they help to predict the net changes that will take place over time within client groups. They can provide correlational knowledge about the association between program intervention and desired changes in program recipients.

The overall validity of this design rests primarily on the assumption that clients and the treatment they receive at each program stage are similar. This assumption is plausible if: (1) eligibility requirements and selection procedures are the same for each group of clients; (2) program content is relatively standard throughout the time period in question; and (3) the client drop-out rate is relatively low (less than 10 percent from the first to the last stage of program processing). Random sampling of clients at each program stage also increases the probability that their characteristics will be similar. Comparison of the social characteristics of the clients in each program phase makes it possible to test this assumption.

As far as internal validity is concerned, the effects of measurement and instrumentation are controlled for by standardization of the data-gathering process for all respondents. Although the effects of history and maturation cannot be controlled for completely, they can be limited by reducing the time intervals between the program stages for which data are gathered.

Regression effects as well can be reduced by taking a number of samples at different times from among those who are awaiting, those who are receiving, and those who have completed treatment. If the data patterns show stability within each sampled group, they would indicate the absence of regression effects.

Finally, the impact of drop-out rates at each stage in the program cycle can be controlled for by assessing drop-out rates at each program stage and comparing the characteristics of those who remain in the program. The more alike the respondent groups are at all stages, the less likely it is that some selective factor controls who drops out and who remains in the program.

REPLICATED CROSS-SECTIONAL SURVEY DESIGNS
AND SOCIAL PROGRAM ADMINISTRATION

Replicated cross-sectional survey designs are only applicable to programs that are cyclic and continuous and that process relatively large numbers of persons. In addition, they require that programs have an ongoing monitoring system to keep accurate records on the numbers and characteristics of clients who complete and drop out of the programs.

These designs can be employed in educational programs, training programs, counseling programs, treatment programs, and so on. While they are not as valid as interrupted time series designs, which document the changes in the same individuals over time, replicated cross-sectional survey designs do provide information regarding the extent to which program intervention appears to be associated with program goals. It provides this information at relatively *low cost* and in a relatively *short space of time*. If no net changes are observed, it can be inferred that the program is not effective with respect to the variables measured. If net changes are observed, during program intervention, it can be inferred that the program probably has an influence on the observed changes.

PRINCIPLES FOR IMPLEMENTING THE REPLICATED CROSS-SECTIONAL SURVEY DESIGN

1. Identifying the Stages in Client Processing

Once it has been determined that the program is cyclic, one must identify the points in the typical sequence of stages through which clients move. These are then regarded as sampling points. A sampling point should be located at the end of each program stage. At a minimum, there should be a sampling point prior to program entry, a sampling point after intervention begins, and a sampling point after intervention ends. Ideally, a number of samples should be drawn at various logical points prior to, during, and after program intervention has been completed.

2. Compiling a List of Persons in Various Program Stages and Monitoring Drop-Out Rates

As we stated earlier, the replicated cross-sectional survey design relies on a sound monitoring system. From agency records one should be able to compile a list of the names and locations of all program recipients at each stage in program processing. In addition, it should be possible to compute the overall drop-out rate for program recipients. If the overall drop-out rate exceeds 10 percent, then this design should be employed with caution and supplemented with a survey of the characteristics of and possible differences between the drop-out population and those who remain. If the drop-outs do not show a net improvement but those who remain in the program do, one might infer an association between intervention and client change. In programs that have a relatively high drop-out rate, however, alternative evaluation designs, such as the interrupted time series, should be employed.

3. Specifying Program Objectives and Selecting Variables for Measuring Effectiveness

In the preceding chapter, we indicated the importance of specifying as precisely as possible the objectives of the program, asking the questions who does what to whom where, when, and why. In conducting a replicated cross-sectional study, it is also important to select outcome measures that are comparable at different points in time. For example, in an alcohol treatment program, asking a person who is awaiting treatment whether treatment has helped reduce his intake of alcohol would make no sense. It would be appropriate, however, to ask program recipients at every stage in such a treatment program questions about their daily intake of alcohol. It is important that measures of program objectives be phrased in terms of variables that *can change* so that changes can be detected among the various time-sampled groups.

Since data are not collected from the same subjects over time, test-retest reliability is not pertinent here. However, since the data in this type of study are likely to be based on self-reports of attitudes, behaviors, and so on, it is important that responses of individual respondents be internally consistent and reliable. Reliability can be achieved by determining whether responses to similar items in the questionnaire or interview are consistent. Thus, if a respondent indicates that he usually has three drinks before dinner and three more before he goes to bed and on another item indicates that he "rarely drinks," one would infer that there is some unreliability in the measures used.

4. Describing the Interventions to Be Evaluated

Next, the program intervention should be described as precisely as possible. The replicated cross-sectional survey design relies on the assumption that all groups, from those who are beginning to receive the intervention to those who have left the program, have received the same program of intervention. If the program has changed markedly, the design is inappropriate and the results invalid. From a study under these circumstances one could not infer an association between the intervention and change. If, however, the intervention is essentially the same for program recipients at all time-sampling points, then one can legitimately employ the replicated cross-sectional survey design.

5. Listing the Persons at Each Sampling Point and Drawing Samples

Separate lists of the names and locations of persons at each phase of the program should then be compiled. As a rough rule of thumb, if the available population at any one stage is less than 50, the total available population should be used. If the population at any one stage exceeds 50, a simple random sample of about 50 should be selected. While more precise estimates of necessary sample sizes can be computed, the above procedures, when used in a program of modest size (for example, approximately 1,000 program recipients per year) would probably provide a fair representation of recipients at each program stage but not so many that it would be too difficult to collect and process the data.

If it is determined that there is a relatively high drop-out rate (over 10 percent) at any stage in the program, one should compile a list of the names and locations of drop-outs. Locating drop-outs is often a difficult and costly process. It may require that additional sources of information be secured such as police, employment, and social security records. It may even be necessary to know several kin, spouse, maternal family names and addresses, and so on. If a relatively complete list of drop-outs is available, a random sample of these should then be selected to serve as an additional comparison group. If program dropouts demonstrate the same degree of change in the desired direction that program recipients do, one could not infer that the program itself was having an impact on its clientele. Alternatively, if drop-outs did not improve but recipients did, one could infer an association between program intervention and client change.

6. Comparing the Background Characteristics of Persons at Different Program Stages

The social characteristics that clients bring to a program can significantly affect the impact of a program on them. For example, the previous job experiences, knowledge, and skills that recipients bring to a job-training program will probably affect the ease with which they learn job skills related to their previous work experience. Social characteristics like age, race, and sex might not have an impact on the acquisition of skills per se but may have an impact on success in job placement. Consequently, in order to determine whether the program itself is having a desired impact, it is necessary to compare the groups at different time periods on those dimensions that might be relevant to the attainment of desired program outcomes. These data should be readily available from existing program records.

If the various groups are relatively comparable, one can infer that differences found on the effectiveness variables between those in early stages and those in later stages of the program are likely to be the product of the program itself. If, however, the relevant social characteristics of the populations in different stages are significantly different, differences found on the effectiveness variables may be a product of the differences in social characteristics.

To test for equivalency of the different time samples, one should first compare the percentage distributions for each relevant social characteristic of the client groups at each stage in program processing. Next, the chi-square statistic should be used to determine whether the time samples are significantly different from each other on each of the socially relevant characteristics. Ideally, one would find *no* significant differences among time samples for each of the socially relevant characteristics.

7. Obtaining Effectiveness Scores for Time-Sampled Groups

The principles articulated in our chapters on questionnaires and interviews should be used to construct standardized instruments for gathering the same effectiveness data from all groups. The cost of the study will be minimized by collecting only data relevant to the achievement of program objectives. However, helpful supplementary data may be obtained from those in the follow-up group(s). These additional questions may involve program recipients' initial expectations of the program, level of satisfaction with the program, ideas about changes that should be made in the program, and so on. Such information can provide program staff with additional ideas about those aspects of the program that require change and those that contribute to program effectiveness.

Gathering data from those who are currently involved in a program or from those who are awaiting involvement is relatively simple. Questionnaires may be handed to them to be filled out or face-to-face interviews can be conducted at the agency itself. From those in the follow-up group or groups, however, data collection is more of a problem. Sometimes, simply locating past program recipients is very costly. Eliciting their cooperation may also be problematic.

If mailed questionnaires are used to gather data from this population, the questionnaires should be as brief as possible and accompanied by a letter soliciting their cooperation. A stamped, self-addressed envelope should also be included. Subsequent inquiries by letter or telephone should be made to encourage nonrespondents to respond. The foregoing techniques promote a high return rate.

Another device for obtaining information from past program participants is the telephone interview. This technique is relatively inexpensive and yields a higher completion rate than the self-administered questionnaire. Obviously, it is only applicable for clients who have telephones.

Finally, if there is a high drop-out rate at any stage in program processing of clientele, it would be useful to find out why. This can be done through telephone interviews or questionnaires sent to program drop-outs. These people should be queried about their reasons for dropping out, under what circumstances they would have continued in the program, and so on. If, by and large, the program shows a low level of effectiveness, such information can be highly suggestive of the changes that should be made to better accomplish program goals.

8. Analyzing and Interpreting the Data

In a replicated cross-sectional survey, the data for each group are aggregated to represent the effects of the program at different stages. To do this, descriptive statistics such as percentages, proportions, means, medians, and modes can be used. If measures of central tendency are used, they should be supplemented with information about the ranges and standard deviations of the distributions at each program stage. In addition, group averages or proportions can be plotted over time on a graph on which the vertical axis is used to represent the effectiveness measure and the horizontal axis to indicate the program stage. For example, figure 11.1 would indicate the proportion of clients at various stages in a three-week smoking clinic who indicate that they currently smoke.

Figure 11.1 indicates no appreciable decline in the proportions of program recipients at each program stage who smoke. Measures of how much they smoke, however, might indicate a significant decline in the amount of smoking. Between any two time points, statistical tests can be employed to deter-

Figure 11.1

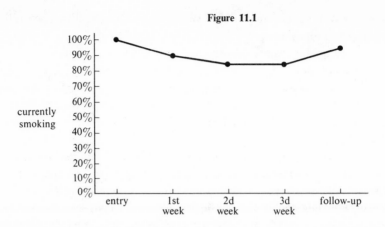

mine whether there are statistically significant changes. For example, one might compare the differences between program entry and program completion to determine whether there was a statistically significant decline in smoking. Here, one would hope to find a *statistically significant change*. However, if one were comparing the proportion smoking at the end of the program with the proportion of smokers in the follow-up group, one would hope to find *no* statistically significant difference. This finding would indicate that the beneficial effects of the program persisted *beyond* program involvement.

HYPOTHETICAL ILLUSTRATION

PROBLEM SITUATION AND ADMINISTRATIVE TASK

An urban YM-YWCA has been conducting a substance abuse education program for high school youth. Participation is voluntary and involves attending weekly classes for two months. There is a waiting list of about 400 youngsters. The program staff can accommodate 50 in each training group and a new group is started every month. Two cohorts of 50 have already completed the program. Prior to this time, there has been no evaluation of the effectiveness of the program. However, a local civic group has indicated a willingness to sponsor an expanded version of the program if it can be demonstrated to be effective. The administrative staff at the ''Y'' now feel that it would be worth the additional investment to evaluate the impact of the ongoing program. A decision is made to conduct a replicated cross-sectional survey of program participants to assess program effectiveness.

1. Identifying the Stages in Client Processing

The program itself is divided into two one-month sections. The first concerns itself with knowledge, attitudes, beliefs, and behaviors related to "soft" drugs and alcohol. The second focuses on knowledge, attitudes, beliefs, and behaviors related to "hard" drugs.

Because of the structure of the program and the fact that two cohorts of 50 have already completed the program, the logical groups for time sampling are those who are awaiting entry into the program, those who are just starting the program, those who are completing the first month, those who are completing the second month, and those who have completed the program. Since there are 400 awaiting entry, a simple random sample of 50 of these youngsters is selected. All those who are currently engaged in the program will be queried. Finally, since there are two cohorts who have "graduated" from the program, one group a month later than the other, these two total groups will be surveyed. The two groups will be analyzed separately to determine whether knowledge, attitudes, beliefs, and behaviors "regress" after participants have been away from the program for a while. Thus, two follow-up groups will be used in the survey.

2. Compiling a List of Persons in Various Program Stages and Monitoring Drop-Out Rates

From agency records it is possible to secure a list of the names and addresses of all potential program recipients who are on the waiting list and of all those who have completed the program. A list of the names of those who are currently in the program is also secured. Only names are necessary for these individuals since they can be given questionnaires or interviews at the "Y."

Next, drop-out rates are computed for the total program and for each program stage. Although it is determined that roughly 6 percent of those awaiting entry do not, in fact, enter the program, virtually all those who enter the program complete it. Hence the overall drop-out rate is relatively low and is not likely to seriously affect estimates of program success. If time and resources permitted, drop-outs might be contacted to determine why they decided not to enter the program after having been on the waiting list. In addition, those on the waiting list might be sampled according to when they are scheduled to enter the program, for example, next month or two months from now. In the present example, however, neither of these two alternatives would be likely to yield information that would justify the additional costs involved.

3. Specifying Program Objectives and Selecting Variables for Measuring Effectiveness

The objectives of the program are to increase knowledge about the properties of drugs and alcohol, to increase knowledge about their physiological effects, to change attitudes about the desirability of using them, and to reduce their usage among program participants.

For the purpose of measurement, a confidential, self-administered questionnaire is constructed that contains a 50-item true-false test tapping respondents' knowledge about alcohol and drugs, items concerning their attitudes about the social desirability of using alcohol and drugs, and items on their current drug and alcohol usage.

The questionnaire is developed in collaboration with the course instructors to determine whether it accurately reflects the content of the course sections. In addition, the questionnaire is pretested with a subsample of 5 youngsters who have completed the program.

The questionnaire itself does not require that respondents give their names or any other identifying information about themselves. This is underscored in the letters mailed to respondents awaiting entry into the program and to those in the follow-up groups. Since the replicated cross-sectional survey design does not involve tracing changes in the same individuals over time, neither names nor identifying codes are necessary. So that the groups from which mailed questionnaires are returned can be determined, the questionnaires are printed on paper of a different color for each group. Questionnaires administered to current program participants are carefully kept in separate piles according to program stage.

4. Describing the Interventions to Be Evaluated

Simultaneously with the development of the questionnaires, program staff are asked to describe in detail the content of the program, the structure of the program, and the objectives and changes that they hope to achieve.

Should the program prove successful, this information will be useful in replicating the program on a wider scale, for hiring additional staff, and so on. Should the program be so successful that other organizations decide to implement similar programs, such detailed descriptions of program content and structure would be invaluable. In the event that the program is unsuccessful or only moderately successful, such detailed description, considered in relation to measured areas of effectiveness and ineffectiveness, can suggest elements of the program that require change.

5. Listing the Persons at Each Sampling Point and Drawing Samples

As we stated earlier, total populations of those currently engaged in the program and of those in the follow-up groups will be employed as "sample" groups. For those awaiting entry, a simple random sample of 50 is selected. Color-coded questionnaires with covering letters and self-addressed, stamped return envelopes are sent to those awaiting entry and to the follow-up groups. Each group of those currently engaged in the program is given questionnaires at the end of the class that marks the end of its phase in the program. Since relatively high return rates were attained with the mailed questionnaires, no reminder letters were sent out.

6. Comparing the Background Characteristics of Persons at Different Program Stages

From registration forms, information about the sex, age, high school grade, race, and religion of participants is available. This background information is analyzed to determine whether the groups studied are comparable along these dimensions. Percentage distributions are compared and chi-squares are computed. From these computations, it is determined that program recipients at each stage of the program are not significantly different in sex composition, age, high school grade, race, and religion. Although no additional background information is available through the questionnaire, at least it can be said that differences in knowledge, attitudes, and drug and alcohol usage are not likely to be the product of differences in the social composition of groups at various program stages. This adds support to the inference that differences found are the product of the program itself.

7. Obtaining Effectiveness Scores for Time Sampled Groups

For each time sampled group the mean score on the 50-item drug and alcohol information test is computed. The data on attitudes toward drug and

Figure 11.2

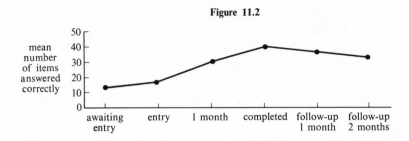

alcohol use and actual current usage are also compiled and aggregated by program phase.

8. Analyzing and Interpreting the Data

The data are then represented on graphs. Figure 11.2 shows the average number of items answered correctly by each time sampled group on the drug and alcohol information test.

The findings indicate a strong increase in knowledge about drugs and alcohol for those who have completed the program. However, the knowledge level drops somewhat in the follow-up groups after "graduation" from the program. On this dimension, then, the program appears to be relatively successful.

Figure 11.3 shows the percentage in each time-sampled group indicating that they agree with the statement: "If you're smart enough you can take any drug and not get hooked." Here we see a desirable decline in the

Figure 11.3

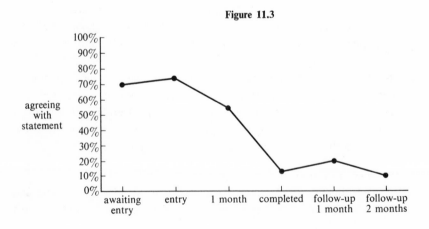

Figure 11.4

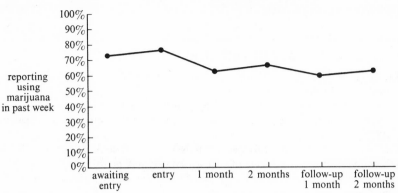

proportion who agree with the statement across program stages. This attitude change persists in the follow-up groups. On this dimension, then, the program is highly successful.

Finally, figure 11.4 shows the proportion of youngsters at each program stage who report that they have used marijuana within the past week. Our data indicate no significant change along this dimension. If reduction of marijuana usage is viewed as a goal of the program, this graph indicates program failure on this dimension. If it is not considered a high priority or a goal of the program, then the finding is not a serious indication of program inefficacy.

Overall, the fact that the different outcome measures yield different patterns attests to the probable validity of the data and to the seriousness with which repondents attended to the task.

These findings and their interpretation were included in an overall evaluation report that was presented to the local civic group for possible additional funding and expansion.

EXERCISE

Select a cyclical educational program that has discernible program stages. Employ a replicated cross-sectional survey design for estimating the extent to which the program is effective in accomplishing its objectives. How would the knowledge gained in such a study compare with the knowledge gained from an interrupted time series study of the same program? Which would be most feasible? Which would be most economical? What inferences could be made from each?

SELECTED BIBLIOGRAPHY

Best, John W. *Research in Education*. 2d ed. Englewood Cliffs, N.J.: Prentice-Hall, 1970; pp. 120–26, 134–36.

Glock, C. Y. "Survey Design and Analysis in Sociology," in C. Y. Glock, ed., *Survey Research in the Social Sciences*. New York: Russell Sage Foundation, 1967; pp. 1–62.

Kahn, A. J. "The Design of Research," in Norman A. Polansky, ed., *Social Work Research*. Chicago: University of Chicago Press, 1960; pp. 61–62.

Suchman, E. A. *Evaluative Research*. New York: Russell Sage Foundation, 1967; pp. 100–2.

Sudman, S. *Reducing the Cost of Surveys*. Chicago: Aldine, 1967, pp. 58–67.

CHAPTER TWELVE

Comparative Experimental Designs

COMPARATIVE EVALUATION DESIGNS are used to assess the relative effectiveness and efficiency of alternative program interventions. They are also used to measure the impact of intervention as compared to nonintervention. The first design involves comparing *two or more* comparable *experimental groups*. In this design, each group received a different program intervention. The second is achieved by comparing an *experimental group* that has received an intervention of some kind with a comparable *control group* that has not. It is possible to combine the elements of both designs. Thus, a program evaluation may involve comparisons between and among comparable experimental groups that have received different interventions and a comparable control group that has received no intervention at all.

The overall validity of comparative designs rests on the assumption that the groups compared are, in fact, comparable. In other words, it is assumed that the only relevant differences between groups are in the program interventions they do or do not receive. This assumption is most likely to be realized when the individuals assigned to each group are assigned *randomly*. However, since random assignment does not insure comparability, the relevant characteristics of each of these groups—that is, those characteristics that are thought to be related to success or failure—should be compared after assignment. This is accomplished by percentage comparisons and computations of chi-squares for each set of characteristics.*

* In addition to reducing the dangers of differential selection, random assignment decreases the dangers of such threats to internal validity as statistical regression and differential experi-

Although the interrupted time series and cross-sectional survey designs discussed in chapters 10 and 11 did not involve comparisons with control groups or with groups that received different program interventions, such comparisons can be built into each of these designs. For example, one can conduct an interrupted time series study of a group that participates in a behavioral smoking clinic and compare it with a comparable control group of smokers who receive no intervention. Here, meaningful inferences about the efficacy of the behavioral program are drawn from before/after comparisons within the group that receives the program intervention and from comparisons between the experimental and control groups after program intervention has been completed.

Likewise, it would be logically possible to add a comparative component to a cross-sectional survey design. Thus, one could conduct a cross-sectional survey of two comparable experimental groups in two different drug education programs. Here again, comparability of the groups is essential. It should be pointed out, however, that comparability is unlikely to occur between programs that are already under way when the decision is made to conduct an evaluation. Moreover, since random assignment to recipient groups is not generally a part of agency policy, even if the two interventions were applied to different groups *within* the same agency, comparability of these groups would be unlikely as well.

In this chapter we focus on *comparative experimental designs*. These designs enable us to assess directly the relative effectiveness and efficiency of two types or degrees of intervention and of intervention and nonintervention. Two elements are essential to comparative experimental designs: (1) random assignment of individual units to experimental and/or control groups; and (2) experimental manipulation of the program intervention(s).*

Comparative experimental designs can be implemented with or without

---

mental mortality. If subjects are randomly selected and assigned to experimental and control groups, the effects of statistical regression and the likelihood of individuals dropping out of each of the groups are assumed to be equally distributed among the groups. Since these factors are not completely controlled for by the randomization process, they require further monitoring during the course of a comparative study.

* Some authors have suggested that intervention programs already under way can be meaningfully compared by simply assuming that these conditions have been approximated. However, in such ex post facto approximations to comparative experimental designs, these assumptions are highly tenuous. Moreover, ex post facto testing of these assumptions is extremely complicated. While the idea of such an experimental approximation may be initially attractive, especially to inexperienced evaluators, we are *not* recommending their use.

Finally, although we have precluded the use of control groups in comparative experiments, some comparisons between experimental groups make it possible to approximate the relative effects of nonintervention without denying services. This is accomplished by varying the amount of a given intervention, measuring effectiveness, and, if there is a linear relationship between the amount of intervention and effectiveness, extrapolating to the nonintervention condition.

For example, figure 12.1 represents the relationship between program effectiveness and three amounts of a single type of intervention (1x, 2x, and 3x). The graph indicates a positive, linear relationship between the amount of intervention and the percentage of program effectiveness. By extending the line to where it intersects with the vertical axis (0x), one can get a rough approximation of the probable level of effectiveness that would be associated with nonintervention.

Varying the amount of input of a single variable, such as number of contacts with clients, time spent in contact with clients, amount of money spent on services to clients, and so on, also makes it possible to estimate the relative efficiency of particular interventions. In the figure 12.1, for example, one can see increase in effectiveness with a proportional increase in program input. Thus, when the amount of intervention is doubled or trebled, the respective level of effectiveness is doubled or trebled. This indicates that each level of intervention is equally efficient.

If however, the study yielded the results represented in figure 12.2, the findings would indicate that although the level of effectiveness increases

Figure 12.1

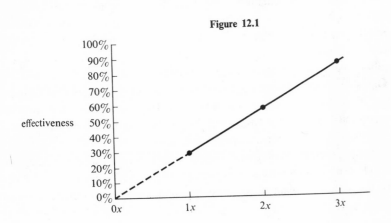

control groups and within and between programs, agencies, or organizations. Our discussion, however, will be restricted to comparative experimental designs that do not employ control groups. In this way, we can avoid the ethical problem of having to deny services to any individuals or groups in order to determine the impact of nonintervention. Meaningful and important comparisons *can* be made between different types or degrees of program intervention without denying services to anyone.

In addition, we are emphasizing the use of comparative experimentation *within* a single program, agency, or organization. Although this restricts our discussion even further, the model that we are advocating does make possible the evaluation of different program strategies, policies, or interventions within programs. Our assumption here is that program administrators will be most likely to employ the model we are presenting.

The hypothetical example we will use illustrates the use of comparative experimentation to evaluate the impact of a program on groups of individual clients, but this approach may also be used to evaluate the impact of alternative personnel policies or supervisory structures on staff performance, the impact of alternative community intervention strategies on different communities, and so on. The ultimate purpose of such a study is to determine which intervention approach works best and at what cost.

A simple schematic representation of our model of comparative experimentation with two experimental groups is presented below. The process takes place sequentially over five different time periods. The time periods are not necessarily equal. First, there is random assignment to experimental groups. Second, evidence is collected regarding the comparability of the experimental groups. Third, effectiveness variables are measured prior to intervention. Fourth, the interventions are introduced and completed. Fifth, effectiveness variables are measured after intervention.

	Time 1	Time 2	Time 3	Time 4	Time 5
	experimental group A	→ establish comparability of groups	→ measure effectiveness variables	→ apply intervention A	→ measure effectiveness variables
random assignment					
	experimental group B	→ establish comparability of groups	→ measure effectiveness variables	→ apply intervention B	→ measure effectiveness variables

Program Evaluation

In this chapter, principles and procedures for comparative evaluation of the effectiveness and efficiency of alternative intervention strategies are discussed. A simple method for determining relative efficiency through cost/effectiveness ratios is also introduced.

COMPARATIVE EXPERIMENTAL DESIGNS AND SOCIAL PROGRAM ADMINISTRATION

Comparative experimentation is most useful when administrative decisions have to be made as to what kinds of personnel are most effective in providing services; how much of a particular kind of service is most effective; which services are most effective and efficient; and so on.

Comparative experimentation is most feasible in relatively complex programs that routinely offer a range of different services that can be manipulated experimentally, in programs that deal with relatively large numbers of clientele, in programs in which clients can be randomly assigned to service groups, and in programs in which desired outcomes are expected within a relatively short period of time, that is, days, weeks, or months.

PRINCIPLES FOR IMPLEMENTING THE COMPARATIVE EXPERIMENTAL DESIGN

1. Identifying Program Objectives

The first step in designing a comparative experiment is to identify those components of a future program that can be manipulated and compared. In order to do this, one must identify program objectives. The questions who does what to whom where, when, and why are again asked, so as to determine possible variations in programming that can yield differences in efficiency or effectiveness.

For example, one might manipulate the dimension of who gives service. Comparisons could be made of the relative effectiveness of professionals as opposed to paraprofessionals, racially matched workers and clients as opposed to unmatched workers and clients, supervisors as opposed to line workers, and so on.

Or, one might manipulate the dimension of what kind of service is given. Comparisons could be made of the relative effectiveness and efficiency of casework and groupwork, psychoanalytic and behavior therapy, transactional analysis groups and gestalt groups, and so on.

One might consider experimentally manipulating the type of clientele the agency serves. Do the same service patterns or interventions work more ef-

fectively and more efficiently with whites or blacks, low-income or middle-income clients, men or women?

Where the program is implemented might be used as well. Clients may be seen in the agency or at home, at their work site or at a clinic after work, in a community center or on the streets. Thus, the relative effectiveness and efficiency of different service locations can be assessed.

Similarly, one might vary *when* services are given. If services are available during the evening are they more likely to be successful than during the day? Are weekend workshops better than weekday workshops?

Finally, one might manipulate and compare interventions on the basis of their intended purposes. Are consciousness raising groups more successful than social action groups? Are drug education programs more successful than programs designed to reduce drug intake of participants?

2. Deciding Which Factors Will Be Manipulated and Compared

Having described the components of the proposed program, one can then decide which program elements will be experimentally manipulated and compared. In the most complicated comparative experiments, *factorial designs* are used to make simultaneous comparisons of the impact of several program elements in various combinations. However, administrators rarely have the resources to conduct such complex studies.

For administrators whose level of research sophistication is not high, we would suggest comparisons of relative *simplicity,* that is, comparisons based on two or three variations on a single dimension. These comparisons are only valid to the extent that all other program components are held constant. Hence it is as important to decide which factors are to be experimentally controlled as it is to decide which factors are to be manipulated and compared. The nonvariation and variation of the respective elements must be carefully monitored throughout the experiment.

One should also choose comparisons that have a clear relation to policy alternatives. Comparisons should not be made just because they would be "interesting" or to satisfy the curiosity of the administrator. They should have a readily identifiable *decision potential.*

A third criterion for choosing comparisons is *manipulability.* Some program elements cannot be legally, ethically, or practically manipulated. Comparisons should be planned for those components over which there is control.

Figure 12.2

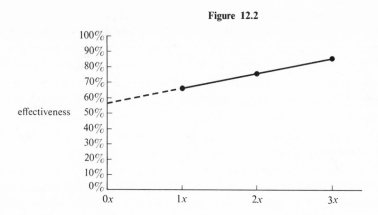

with increased program input, the increase in one is not proportional to the increase in the other. In fact, the graph indicates that of all the amounts of intervention, the lowest, 1*x*, is the most efficient, since it yields the highest amount of effectiveness for the input.

3. Specifying Target Population and Sample

Next, one should describe the characteristics of the target population that the program is intended to serve and devise a strategy for selecting a sample for participation in the comparative experiment. To the extent possible, the sample should be representative of the target population. This is particularly important with respect to characteristics that may be associated with different degrees of success in the program. Thus, if sampling is employed, it should be random sampling. In addition, percentage comparisons and chi-squares should be computed to determine whether the differences between the target population and the sample are statistically significant. If clients cannot be selected by random sampling, percentage comparisons should still be made between the target population and actual program clients to see if they are similar on relevant characteristics. If the entire target population participates in the program, representativeness is, of course, not an issue.

4. Operationally Defining Program Objectives

Operational definition of program objectives is necessary for assessing program outcomes. For adequate comparisons, the program units compared should have the same objectives. Sometimes, however, objectives are not completely congruent. In such cases, comparisons are made primarily on common objectives. Secondarily, however, by comparing levels of effectiveness achieved on objectives that are *not* shared, one can use units that do not share the objective as approximations to a control group.

The main principle here is that variables should be selected that can be employed to measure changes for the units that are being compared. This is most problemmatic when different *types* of program content are being experimentally manipulated and compared. It is least problematic when the same content is employed in different amounts, in different locations, by different providers, and so on.

The criteria for selecting measures of effectiveness are the same as those discussed in connection with interrupted time series and cross-sectional survey designs. The measures should be sensitive to change, reliable, valid, and related to program objectives.

Finally, some information might be gathered regarding possible undesirable outcomes. Thus, drug education classes may have the undesirable side-effect of encouraging some youngsters to experiment with drugs. If an evaluation of classes taught by different instructors only measured the acquisition of information about drugs and did not assess changes in patterns of drug use (even though such changes were not a goal of the program), extremely important information about the effects of the different classes would be lost.

5. Developing Forms for Monitoring Costs of Program Variations

In order to determine the relative efficiency of different program inputs, information about their relative costs must be collected. In those comparative experiments in which costs do not vary, only effectiveness need be assessed. For example, in a study of short-term versus long-term psychotherapy, relative costs can be readily established. Alternatively, in a study of the comparative effectiveness of racially matched and racially unmatched therapists and clients, costs are presumed to be constant. In the latter study, only relative effectiveness need be measured.

When possible, information about the amount of program resources, staff time, equipment, transportation, and so on should be collected through standard monitoring forms for the various program interventions compared. The procedures for developing forms were discussed in chapters 6 and 7.

Cost data are used for developing *cost/effectiveness ratios*. These ratios express the relative efficiency of one or another intervention. They are based on measures of effectiveness divided by the cost of program inputs. For example, two delinquency prevention units may have the same degree of success. Each demonstrates a 30 percent recidivism rate for its participants six months after completion of the program. However, one unit spends $1,000 per youngster as compared to $6,000 for the other unit. The cost/effectiveness ratios for these programs are 70%/$1,000 versus 70%/$6,000. With equal effectiveness but different costs, the former, less costly program is clearly the most efficient.*

6. Allocating Program Recipients to Experimental Groups

Having completed the five preceding steps, one can begin to implement the experiment. This involves allocating program recipients to the various comparison groups. Ideally, this should be done *randomly* to maximize the probability of comparability: each program recipient should have an equal probability of being assigned to each comparison group. This can be done with the flip of a coin, table of random numbers, and so on.

When random assignment is not possible, *systematic assignment* might be used. In this approach, subjects are assigned to experimental groups on a rotating basis. For example, if there are three comparison groups, the first client to enter a program goes into group 1, the second into group 2, the third into group 3, the fourth into group 1, and so on.

If neither of the foregoing techniques is feasible, *block assignment* may be used. Here, blocks of subjects are assigned to comparison groups. For example, the first 25 to apply to a program go into group 1, the second 25 into group 2, and so on.

Under no circumstances, however, should staff be allowed to assign or to influence the assignment of individuals to experimental groups. Staff are inclined to do this out of a desire to see to it that program recipients receive the services that staff think will most benefit the recipients. Or, they may assign clientele on the basis of self-interest, choosing clients for their own groups who are in some ways most desirable. Irrespective of staff motives, this practice introduces an uncontrollable bias into the allocation process. *No*

---

* It should be clear to the reader that we are *not* discussing cost/benefit analysis here. The latter involves translating effectiveness information into dollars and cents. This is a highly complex technique, which relies on many, sometimes tenuous assumptions. A full discussion of this technique falls outside the scope of this book.

meaningful comparisons can be made between groups thus constituted. Many a comparative experiment has been completely ruined by this form of unintended subversion. In order to safeguard against this, procedures for allocation must be completely beyond the reach of program staff.

Whatever the allocation procedure, it is important to check for comparability of the groups on variables that might influence the outcome measures. Here again, percentage comparisons and chi-squares are computed to insure that the differences between the comparison groups on these variables are *not* statistically significant.

Generally speaking, 25 to 50 subjects should be assigned to each experimental group. This number will keep the data within manageable limits. Groups of less than 25 are too small for meaningful comparisons.

7. Taking Effectiveness Scores Prior to Intervention

Once subjects have been allocated to experimental groups, their scores on the effectiveness measures should be collected. As noted in the previous two chapters, the measures themselves should be standardized. Measurement procedures must be the same for all experimental groups.

These "before" measurements are essential in experiments in which random allocation is not used. They establish the comparability of the experimental groups on the outcome measures. In so doing, they make it possible to infer that differences obtained *after* intervention were not the consequence of differences between experimental groups *before* intervention.

Whatever the method of subject allocation, comparisons between pre- and postintervention measurements make it possible to control for the effects of statistical regression and differential selection. Ideally then, preintervention measurements should be taken in *all* comparative experiments to establish firmly the comparability of experimental groups and the validity of inferences about the impact of intervention.

Sometimes, however, taking such measurements is not feasible. Or, it might unduly influence the subjects' awareness of the objectives of the study. The latter is referred to as *measurement effects*. In studies in which this potential bias is a major concern, preintervention measurements may be taken in some experimental groups but not in others to determine whether the "before" measurements themselves have influenced the scores on the outcome measures.

8. Implementing the Intervention Strategies

At this point, the intervention strategies should be implemented. Interventions should be standardized so that only intended differences exist between interventions received by the different experimental groups. All other aspects of the interventions should be identical.

It is also important that the interventions employed with the different experimental groups are not *contaminated*. This means that staff serving one experimental group should not begin introducing techniques intended for another experimental group. Such contamination makes it impossible to assess the effects of different types of intervention because the original differences in interventions received by the experimental groups have been obscured.

In order to guard against the foregoing dangers, staff activities should be monitored closely to insure that the experimental groups are receiving *only* those interventions that they are supposed to receive. In addition, the quality of the interventions should be monitored. Depending on resources and the degree of rigor desired, this monitoring may involve the use of staff activity forms, observational studies, or less formal approaches. Whatever the method, some form of monitoring is essential to insure that the study is assessing the effectiveness and efficiency of the intended interventions.

9. Measuring Effectiveness after Intervention

After the interventions have been fully implemented, effectiveness data should be collected. However, it is important to decide *when* postintervention measurements should be taken. This decision requires serious attention and is based on program expectations, issues of cost, and the potential accessibility of participants after program completion. In general, comparative experimentation is most useful for measuring interventions and changes over relatively short time periods, for example, less than six months. Programs that extend over relatively long periods of time are subject to the risks of high drop-out rates, high staff turnover, and difficulties in maintaining the standardization of interventions.

In *after-only* comparative experiments, where only postintervention effectiveness measurements are taken, it is again essential that the measurement procedures used be standardized. In *before/after* comparative experiments, effectiveness measures should be standardized over time as well. In other words, the same measurement procedures should be used for all experimental groups *before* and *after* program intervention.

10. Collecting, Analyzing, and Interpreting the Data

Once the data have been collected, it is possible to determine the relative effectiveness of the intervention strategies being compared. In after-only studies, percentage comparisons, comparisons of mean scores, and so on are made between the experimental groups. Chi-squares may be computed to determine whether differences in the effectiveness scores of these groups are statistically significant. The groups with effectiveness scores that are significantly higher have received the more effective intervention.

In before/after studies, comparisons are made *within* experimental groups over time as well as *between* experimental groups. Before/after comparisons within a group indicate the impact of the intervention on that group itself. Comparisons of postintervention scores *between* experimental groups indicate the degree of success achieved by each intervention strategy. Comparisons of the before/after changes *between* experimental groups yield the most precise indication of the relative effectiveness of the various interventions.

After the effectiveness data have been analyzed, questions of relative efficiency should be raised. The costs of implementing the various interventions should be determined. Finally, cost/effectiveness ratios should be computed for each intervention.

Decisions about future program interventions should be based on relative effectiveness, relative efficiency, and, if possible, information about any undesirable side-effects of implementing specific interventions.

HYPOTHETICAL ILLUSTRATION

PROBLEM SITUATION AND ADMINISTRATIVE TASK

Social work staff in an adoption agency have the responsibility for screening and selecting potential adoptive parents, informing them about agency procedures, informing them about legal aspects of adoption, matching children with adoptive parents, and observing the progress of children who are placed for adoption.

In this agency, there is a long list of prospective adoptive parents awaiting agency processing. Since there is a relatively small supply of children available for adoption, and the agency's routine, one-to-one casework processing of each set of applicants takes about six months to complete, applications experience a high level of frustration and anxiety in the process. Moreover, the present "first come, first served" policy gives much more significance to when a client couple applies than to their relative merits as potential adoptive parents compared to those of other couples in the current client pool.

Sensitive to these problems, the agency director has decided to try a group approach to certain aspects of client processing. By dividing the functions of social work staff into those that can be appropriately accomplished in groups and those that require work with couples individually, he is able to plan a program intervention that will hopefully accomplish program goals in less time and with greater client satisfaction than do present operating procedures. So that the relative effectiveness and efficiency of the new approach can be evaluated, a comparative experiment is designed.

1. Identifying Program Objectives

The overall program objectives include everything from screening and selecting potential adoptive parents to supervising the progress of children who have been placed for adoption. More specifically, the program goals to which the group approach is directed are as follows: (1) to inform applicants about agency policies and procedures; (2) to inform applicants about legal aspects of adoption; (3) to reduce the amount of staff time devoted to providing the foregoing information; (4) to increase the amount of staff time devoted to other social work functions; (5) to reduce the waiting time for determining the eligibility of applicants; (6) to increase the number of couples considered within a given time period; and (7) to increase the level of client satisfaction with the program.

2. Deciding Which Factors Will Be Manipulated and Compared

Although the director has considered the possibility of using volunteers or paraprofessionals to orient applicants, he decides that it would be least disruptive to the agency to begin by having existing professional staff attempt a group approach. He has considered using a written agency "handout" to accomplish the orientation, but staff have been highly resistant to that approach. He decides that simply contrasting a group with an individual approach to orientation would be most productive and least disruptive. In this experiment, two comparable applicant groups will be compared, one receiving group orientation and the other, individual orientation. All other aspects of the program remain the same. No staff changes ae made. In subsequent efforts, other aspects of the program might be experimented with.

3. Specifying Target Population and Sample

The target population consists of all couples who apply to the program within a period of three months, approximately one hundred couples. The entire target population will be included in the study and sampling will be unnecessary.

4. Operationally Defining Program Objectives

On the basis of the objectives identified earlier, various measures of the impact of the orientation program on client knowledge and attitudes are developed. They range from pencil-and-paper tests of client knowledge of agency procedures and legal aspects of adoption to scales measuring client anxiety, satisfaction with service, attitudes toward agency procedures, and so on.

A decision is made *not* to attempt to measure the impact of this intervention on the success of adoptive placements. This would require a wait of over a year to assess impact. If that were the major objective, a cross-sectional survey design might be used.

5. Developing Forms for Monitoring Costs of Program Variations

To determine the relative efficiency of group and individual orientation procedures, staff activity forms are developed to monitor the amount of staff time spent in orientation and in other activities per applicant couple, the numbers of couples fully processed within the three-month time period, and the length of time it took applicants to complete their processing for eligibility. Since the staff members doing group and individual orientation are of equal status, get the same salaries, and require no special equipment, the two approaches involved the same direct monetary outlay. Thus, differences in efficiency are based on time spent with clientele, numbers of clients seen, cases completed, and the like.

6. Allocating Program Recipients to Experimental Groups

To maximize the likelihood of comparability between the experimental groups, the director assigns couples to individual or to group orientation randomly, by flipping a coin. Two experimental groups of about fifty couples each are assigned in this way. By comparison of percentage distributions and computation of chi-squares, it is established that the experimental groups do not differ significantly on age, race, level of education, income, religion, or present size of family.

Moreover, to maximize the likelihood that quality of staff is the same for both experimental groups, social workers are assigned randomly to do group or individual orientation. If this becomes a problem, workers can be rotated so that all do some individual and some group orientation. The workers themselves, however, have no control over whether a particular applicant receives group or individual orientation.

7. Taking Effectiveness Scores Prior to Intervention

When applicants first come into the program, they are given a short questionnaire to complete along with their application. On this questionnaire are items that test applicants' knowledge of agency procedures, legal aspects of adoption, and expectations of the agency. Couples are encouraged to complete the questionnaire as a couple. Having these measures prior to intervention makes it possible to know how effective the orientation is as well as whether applicants enter the program with a high level of knowledge about areas covered by the orientation. If the latter were true, it would suggest that an orientation program was not necessary for most applicants.

8. Implementing the Intervention Strategies

Once a sufficient number of applicants has come to the agency, group and individual appointments are set up. A standardized group orientation program is developed to compare with the already standardized individual orientation approach. Efforts are made throughout the experiment to see to it that social workers are approaching these tasks in a relatively consistent manner.

9. Measuring Effectiveness after Intervention

After three months, postintervention effectiveness measurements are taken. Applicants again complete short questionnaires concerning their knowledge of agency procedures, legal aspects of adoption, and so on. In addition, they will indicate their present level of satisfaction with agency service.

Other relevant data will then be collected through the staff monitoring forms.

10. Collecting, Analyzing, and Interpreting the Data

Once all the questionnaires and forms are completed, the data are tabulated. Before and after comparisons are made of the group receiving group orientation and the group receiving individual orientation. The data reveal that both orientation procedures produce the same level of knowledge. Hence they do not differ in their effectiveness.

The staff monitoring data do reveal, however, that group orientation is more efficient than individual orientation. On the average, it takes those applicants who receive group orientation significantly less time to complete the eligibility process. In addition, social workers are able to see more applicants during the same time period. Finally, a comparison is made between the social characteristics of those who are judged acceptable as adoptive parents and those who are not in each experimental group. On these dimensions, whether a couple receives individual or group orientation is not influencing social workers' decisions about who should be an adoptive parent and who should not. Hence group orientation produces results similar to individual orientation, but it does so much more efficiently.

EXERCISE

Visit a public welfare agency. Determine the stated objectives of a specific program and the procedures employed to achieve these objectives. Consider which program dimensions might be experimentally manipulated. Select one of these dimensions and devise a comparative experiment to evaluate the relative effectiveness and efficiency of alternative intervention approaches.

SELECTED BIBLIOGRAPHY

Glaser, D. *Routinizing Evaluation*. Rockville, Md.: National Institute of Mental Health, Center for Studies of Crime and Delinquency, 1973; pp. 26–47, 74–79.
Hyman, H. H., and C. R. Wright. "Evaluating Social Action Programs," in P. F. Lazarsfeld, W. H. Sewell, and H. L. Wilensky, eds., *The Uses of Sociology*. New York: Basic Books, 1967; pp. 741–82.

Hyman, H. H., C. R. Wright, and T. K. Hopkins. *Applications of Methods of Evaluation*. Berkeley: University of California Press, 1962; pp. 20–29, 40–54.

McLean, P. D. "Evaluating Community-Based Psychiatric Services," in P. O. Davidson, F. W. Clark, and L. A. Hamerlynck, eds., *Evaluation of Behavioral Programs*. Champaign, Ill.: Research Press, 1974; pp. 83–102.

Riecken, H. W., and R. F. Boruch, eds. *Social Experimentation*. New York: Academic Press, 1974; pp. 3–43, 108–13.

Weiss, Carol H. *Evaluation Research*. Englewood Cliffs, N.J.: Prentice-Hall, 1972; pp. 78–85.

CHAPTER THIRTEEN

Crossover Designs

THE COMPARATIVE EXPERIMENTAL DESIGNS discussed in the preceding chapter have two major limitations. First, they require that experimental groups receive different interventions or different degrees of the same intervention if meaningful comparisons are to be made. When different interventions are employed, every experimental group in the study is denied the intervention received by every other experimental group. If a single intervention strategy is applied in different degrees to two different experimental groups, it means that one group is necessarily receiving less intervention than the other. This denial of a type or of an amount of intervention may be ethically and professionally unacceptable in some programs. Probably, it is only justifiable in social agencies when it can be safely said that we have no idea whether one type, degree, or combination of interventions is better than any other.

In addition, service recipients may object to the differences in the kinds or degrees of services they receive. Understandably, they are interested in receiving all the services they possibly can. As a result they may object to the service denial and drop out of the program. Or, they may seek elsewhere the services denied to them. The former would increase the problems of experimental mortality, and the latter would invalidate comparisons between experimental groups in the study.

The second major limitation of comparative experimental designs is that they do not allow for control group comparisons without complete denial of services to some agency clientele. For ethical, professional, and practical reasons, we rejected the use of such control groups in social program evaluation.

Crossover comparative experimental designs make it possible to compare the relative impacts of different intervention strategies *without* denying any of the interventions to any of the experimental groups. In a crossover evaluation, comparable groups of clients are given different interventions, impact is measured, and then the kinds of interventions received by the experimental groups are "crossed over" or switched, and impact is again measured. As a result, the effectiveness of every intervention strategy on every experimental group is assessed. This provides a greater number of comparisons than in noncrossover designs, and *equal* services are given to *all* experimental groups. The only differences between the groups are in *when* they receive which intervention.

By building into the crossover design a time lag in the implementation of interventions to different experimental groups, it is possible to conduct a quasi–control group evaluation in a social agency without denying any of the full range of interventions to any client group.

Finally, by using crossover and time lag techniques, one can conduct a *true* control group evaluation in a social agency without denying intervention to any client group. In other words, one can study the effects of intervention in comparison with nonintervention on *all* client groups. In such *time-lagged crossover control group* designs, all client groups constitute experimental or control groups at various points in time. By the end of the study, however, each group has received a complete range of interventions.

Time-lagged crossover control group evaluations can be conducted with more than two comparison groups and with more than one intervention strategy, but the basic elements of the design are presented below in a schematic representation employing two comparison groups and a single intervention strategy.

	Time 1	Time 2	Time 3	Time 4	Time 5
group A	→ measure outcome variables	→ intervention	→ measure outcome variables	→ no intervention	→ measure outcome variables
random assignment group B	→ measure outcome variables	→ no intervention	→ measure outcome variables	→ intervention	→ measure outcome variables

In the time-lagged crossover control design presented above, two comparable groups of clients are randomly assigned. Both groups are measured on the outcome variables prior to intervention at time 1. At time 2, group A receives the program intervention while group B does not. At this point in time, group A is serving as an experimental group, while group B serves as a control group. At time 3, outcome measures are again taken. At time 4, the intervention "crossover" takes place whereby group B receives the experimental intervention and group A becomes a control group, receiving no intervention. Finally, at time 5, outcome measures are taken for a third time.

Comparisons of the group scores on the outcome measures are made at times 1, 3, and 5. Comparisons at time 1 indicate the comparability of the two groups on the outcome measures prior to intervention. Before/after comparisons at time 3, within and between groups A and B, give the first indication of program effectiveness and are identical to the comparisons that would be made in a classical experimental study. Comparisons within group B between times 3 and 5 would replicate the experiment with group B. Within the latter two time periods the differences observed within group A would indicate whether the positive effects of intervention diminished after intervention was terminated. Finally, comparisons between group A at time 3 and group B at time 5 would indicate whether both groups had achieved the same desired levels of change as a result of program intervention.

One major advantage of the time-lagged crossover control design is that within it all internal validity factors are controlled. Randomization of group assignment controls for the differential selection of subjects and for statistical regression effects. The use of control groups limits the effects of contemporary history and maturation processes. The potential effects of pretesting are reduced by using standardized measures for assessing the control groups at times 1 and 3. Moreover, in this design, the effects of experimental mortality are easily monitored. Although the interaction effects of all of the foregoing factors cannot be precisely delineated, those effects are decreased by randomization, experimental and control group comparisons, and by the built-in replication that occurs between times 3 and 5. This replication also makes it possible to infer that findings that are consistent throughout the experiment may be generalized to other comparable programs within the agency in which the study was conducted.

TIME-LAGGED CROSSOVER CONTROL DESIGNS AND SOCIAL PROGRAM ADMINISTRATION

The design discussed above is most useful for determining the effectiveness of a program intervention when there are large numbers of clients desiring the intervention; when all of these clients cannot receive the service simultaneously, necessitating a waiting list; when program interventions are expected to have results in a relatively short period of time; and when the desired outcomes of program intervention can be clearly specified. The unique advantage of this design is that it provides the scientific rigor of a control group experiment without requiring any service denial to any agency clients.

PRINCIPLES FOR IMPLEMENTING THE TIME-LAGGED CROSSOVER CONTROL GROUP DESIGN

1. Identifying and Operationally Defining Program Objectives

Along the lines suggested in the previous chapters, program objectives should be identified and converted into standardized measurement procedures and instruments. Here, as with previously discussed designs, multiple measures of desired outcomes are preferable.

Within the context of this design, it is important to specify when the desired changes are expected to occur. These expected times indicate when outcome measurements should be taken. If the time period is too long—over three months, for example—this design becomes unwieldy and subject to high rates of client drop-out. If appropriate time intervals cannot be specified, this design should not be used. In the latter case, a less rigorous design, such as the interrupted time series, should be used.

2. Determining the Acceptability of Time-Lagged Control Groups

Since this design requires the use of time-lagged control groups, it is important to determine whether the agency climate is one in which even these requirements are ethically and practically acceptable to staff and clientele. This is generally not a problem when there is a waiting list for service and when staff and clientele alike understand that all client groups will receive a full complement of services. Nevertheless, the time-lag aspect of the design does require that some clients, randomly selected, receive services sooner than others. This may present a problem. If it is not fully acceptable to all concerned, this randomization process may be undermined by staff, or clients may drop out or simultaneously seek services elsewhere. Each of these possibilities could seriously jeopardize the validity of the evaluation.

3. Defining and Standardizing the Intervention

For true comparisons between experimental and control groups and a true replication, interventions should be standardized with respect to content, technology, time, personnel, and so on. Both experimental groups must receive the same intervention for generalizations to be made. Provision should be made for monitoring program interventions at times 2 and 4 to determine their comparability.

4. Specifying Target Population and Sample

As indicated in the discussions of previous evaluation designs, the target population and sample should be specified. The representativeness of the sample should be assessed. Data concerning the characteristics of the sample are also useful for identifying the types of clients with whom the program is most effective.

5. Allocating Program Recipients to Experimental and Control Groups

Having completed the four previous steps, one can begin actually implementing the experiment. This involves allocating program recipients to the initial experimental and control groups. As with comparative experimental designs, random assignment to groups is preferable. If this is not feasible, systematic allocation is an acceptable but less desirable option. Finally, block assignment may be used if neither of the other methods is possible. Whatever the method of allocation used, the comparability of the comparison groups must be checked, and staff should have no influence over the allocation process.

6. Taking Effectiveness Scores Prior to Intervention

Once the groups are assigned and comparability is established, group scores on the effectiveness measures should be taken. These measurement procedures and instruments should be standardized throughout the study.

7. Implementing the Intervention

After preintervention measures have been taken, the intervention strategy may be implemented. It is especially important here to keep the experimental and control groups separate and distinct. *Leakage* occurs when those who receive the program intervention interact with those in the control group so that there is diffusion of the intervention from one group to the other. Such contamination of the control group makes it impossible to assess the actual impact of the intervention. In the time-lagged crossover control design, one must guard against leakage during the second phase of the study as well. Thus, after the crossover one must guard against contamination of the "new" control group.

8. Measuring Effectiveness after Intervention

With the same procedures and instruments used prior to intervention, a set of postintervention measurements should be taken. Comparisons are made between the experimental and control groups. These initial comparisons provide the first assessments of program effectiveness. If there are no differences between comparison groups at time 3, the design should probably be discontinued. If, however, there is reason to believe that the intervention had no discernible effect because it was implemented for too short a duration, one might extend the time period and the amount of program intervention. Naturally, a comparable adjustment would be made in the intervention applied during the second phase of the study, that is, between times 3 and 5.

9. Implementing the Intervention with the Former Control Group.

If differences are noted between comparison groups during the first phase of the study, program intervention should now be implemented with the group that was previously the control group. This intervention should be identical to the intervention used in the first phase of the study. Leakage is less of a problem during this second phase, since at that time all clients are expected to have received the intervention. However, the validity of the replication will be diminished to the extent that the new control group receives additional intervention through contamination. This could create a false impression that clients continue to change in a desirable direction after termination or that clients maintain their gains after intervention has been terminated.

10. Collecting Analyzing and Interpreting Effectiveness Data after the Second Intervention Phase

At the end of the specified intervention period, effectiveness scores are again taken and the data are analyzed for all comparison groups for all time periods. The results of such comparisons would indicate the effectiveness of program intervention with both comparison groups and the consistency of impact. If the findings indicate a consistent, desirable change for both groups then it would be safe to infer that the intervention is demonstrated to be effective *within* the agency or program.

Hypothetical Illustration

PROBLEM SITUATION AND ADMINISTRATIVE TASK

An administrator in a junior high school wants to implement a reading tutorial program for students who are reading at least a year below grade level. He decides to recruit high school volunteers as tutors and would like to assess the impact of the program on his students' reading skills.

After recruiting 20 volunteer tutors, he arranges for each to undergo a short period of training. Each tutor agrees to provide a ten-week tutorial for one junior high school student, to be followed by a second ten-week tutorial for a second student. In this way, 40 students can receive tutorial help. The cost of such a program is minimal. A time-lagged crossover control group study will be used to determine the program's effectiveness.

1. Identifying and Operationally Defining Program Objectives

The program objective is to improve the reading skills of students who are reading at least one year below grade level. This objective will be assessed in terms of standardized reading speed, reading comprehension, and reading grade level. It is anticipated that changes on all of these dimensions will take place as a result of the ten-week tutorial period.

2. Determining the Acceptability of Time- Lagged Control Groups

Since there are many more students in need of tutorial help than there are tutors, both school staff and students alike accept a waiting list and random assignment to experimental and control groups. There is some agitation from teachers to provide tutorials for those students whose reading skills are poorest. However, the administrator is concerned that these students may not be able to benefit from nonprofessional tutorial help. As a result, it would be best to have students representing a range of reading deficiency to determine with whom such a program works best.

3. Defining and Standardizing the Intervention

Tutors are exposed to a standardized training program and observed in role play tutorials to see to it that some standardization is achieved in the content of their tutorials. The time, place, and duration of tutorials is also standardized. Since the same tutors will be used twice during the study, a certain amount of standardization of personnel is achieved. This is, however, possibly offset by the "practice effect" of giving two sets of tutorials.

In other words, tutors may be better the second time around. This would be indicated by a greater change between times 3 and 5 than between times 1 and 3.

4. Specifying Target Population and Sample

In the junior high school, the target population of students who read at least one year below grade level numbers 120. Since the program makes provision for 40 students, a random sample of one-third of the target population is selected. These 40 are not significantly different from the target population on variables such as age, school grade, reading level, sex, and race. Hence on these variables the sample is representative.

5. Allocating Students to Experimental and Control Groups

The 40 students are then randomly assigned to an experimental and a control group, each containing 20 students. These groups are found to be comparable on age, school grade, reading level, sex, and race.

6. Taking Effectiveness Scores Prior to Intervention

Before the tutorials begin, students' reading speed, level of comprehension, and reading grade level are assessed and recorded. The groups should be comparable on these scores as well.

7. Implementing the Intervention

At this point, the tutorial program begins with the 20 students assigned to the experimental group. Those assigned to the control group receive no tutorial assistance. It is also determined that none of the youngsters in the control group are receiving "outside" tutorials.

8. Measuring Effectiveness after Intervention

With the same measure of reading skills used prior to intervention, a new set of measurements is taken after 10 weeks of tutorials have been completed. Initial comparisons between experimental and control groups indicate a positive change in reading speed but no change in reading comprehension or reading grade level.

9. Implementing the Intervention with the Former Control Group

After the second set of effectiveness measurements has been taken, tutorials are begun with the second group of 20 students. As much as possible, the same tutorial methods are used as before. Tutorials with the first set of students are terminated.

10. Collecting, Analyzing, and Interpreting Effectiveness Data

A final set of effectiveness scores is taken after the second ten-week tutorial program has been completed. These are compared with measurements taken prior to intervention and after the first set of interventions. The final set of comparisons indicates a positive change in reading comprehension and in reading grade level as well as in reading speed. This suggests a possible "practice effect" for tutors, that is, their experiences may be improving their tutorial skills. Finally, an analysis of the characteristics of those students who seem to benefit most from the program indicates that those who are reading between one and two years below grade level receive the most benefit from the tutorial programs; these students show the greatest improvement after the intervention of tutorials. Those whose reading grade level is more than two years below grade level seem to derive no benefit from the tutorial program. For them, more professional assistance is probably in order.

EXERCISE

Devise a time-lagged crossover control group design for a training program in a public health agency. Specify the program objectives in measurable terms. Indicate the program intervention to be used and the target population with whom it will be used. What professional, practical, and ethical considerations arise in implementing such a study?

SELECTED BIBLIOGRAPHY

Gottman, J. M., and S. R. Leiblum. *How to Do Psychotherapy and How to Evaluate It.* New York: Holt, Rinehart, and Winston, 1974; pp. 138–51.

Gottman, J. M., R. M. McFall, and J. T. Barnett. "Design and Analysis of Research Using Time Series," *Psychological Bulletin,* 72, no. 4 (1969), 299–306.

Hall, R. V. et al. "Modification of Behavior Problems in the Home with a Parent as Observer and Experimenter," *Journal of Applied Behavioral Analysis* 5 (Spring 1972), 53–64.

Riecken, H. W., and R. F. Boruch, eds. *Social Experimentation.* New York: Academic Press, 1974; pp. 41–86.

Weiss, Carol H. *Evaluation Research.* Englewood Cliffs, N.J.: Prentice-Hall, 1972; pp. 60–66.

CHAPTER FOURTEEN

Summary and Conclusions

IN THIS BOOK, we have attempted to show how research principles, techniques, and knowledge can be applied to program planning, monitoring, and evaluation by administrators and planners. Although we separated planning, monitoring, and evaluation for purposes of discussion, we recognize that these functions are interdependent. Thus, sound program planning is a necessary precursor to effective program monitoring. Valid and reliable monitoring information is necessary for effective program evaluation, and competent program evaluation can serve as a basis for a new cycle of program planning and implementation.

Similarly, for the sake of clarity, we have somewhat arbitrarily discussed different research techniques in the context of different administrative functions. Thus, the techniques of questionnaire construction, interviewing, assessing research reports, and observation were discussed in the context of program planning. These techniques might just as easily have been applied to problems of program monitoring or program evaluation. Conducting a census, form construction, sampling, and data analysis were discussed in the context of program monitoring. These techniques might just as easily have been applied to problems of program planning and evaluation. Although the various formative evaluation designs discussed in the last section of the book are generally used to assess the impact of program intervention, they may be used as well to evaluate the relative effectiveness and efficiency of different planning efforts. Consequently, throughout the book we argue for the creative and flexible application of these techniques to different areas of administrative decision making.

Furthermore, we contend that research techniques and the knowledge they generate can augment administrative rationality. This is especially true when information is gathered with particular decisions in mind. If the administrator himself is designing the study, he should consider from the start the decision-making implications of different possible findings. If the study is designed by an outside research consultant or by inside research staff, an understanding of the research techniques employed and the programmatic implications of various possible findings is essential to the administrator. Where this understanding is lacking, researchers are less likely to be held accountable by the administrator, and the research itself is less likely to be administratively useful.

THE SCOPE AND LIMITS OF THE BOOK

Ours was a modest attempt to introduce research techniques and principles to administrators and planners with no previous research training. Our examples were confined to relatively small, relatively simple programs and agencies. As a result, we have not discussed the more sophisticated research techniques and modalities that are used in large, highly complex social programs and agencies. Cost accounting, cost/benefit analysis, computer applications, complex information systems, and systems analysis were considered beyond the scope of this book. Superficial coverage of these subjects would have been worse than no coverage at all.

Moreover, within the realm of social research, we did not discuss summative evaluation techniques for generating cause-effect knowledge that would be generalizable beyond a particular program or agency. This type of research requires a high level of expertise. And, it should be pointed out, efforts by researchers to produce such "universal" knowledge have not been all that successful.

Rather, we have attempted to illustrate how formative evaluations can assist program planners and administrators in making decisions *within* specific programs or agencies. This form of social research, which is potentially most useful to program administrators and planners, has generally been neglected by researchers, research consultants, and research educators.

NEXT STEPS FOR THE READER

After learning and applying the research principles and techniques presented in this book, the reader may want to pursue other, related sources of knowledge. These sources include: the design of information processing systems;

the uses of computers for storing, retrieving, and analyzing program information; systems analysis; advanced statistical methods; and cost/benefit
analysis.

Even administrators who do not choose to acquire knowledge about more
sophisticated research techniques and procedures may employ staff or research consultants who advocate their use. We would recommend that such
administrators learn enough about these techniques and procedures to know
what can properly be expected from them. Without this knowledge, administrators have occasionally discovered that they have invested considerable amounts of scarce organizational resources in research projects that
have provided little programmatic return on their investment.

Index

DATE DUE

FEB 7 1980			
MAR 0 6 1980			